Helmi Mavis: A Finnish-American Girlhood

Mavis Hiltunen Biesanz

North Star Press of St. Cloud, Inc.

The photos of the Rex Theater on page 53; the Main Street of Tower, Minnesota, on page 54; a Fourth of July parade in Tower, Minnesota, on page 61; the Tower high school on page 103; and the Finnish Temperance Hall on page 133 are used courtesy of the Iron Range Research Center, Tower-Soudan Historical Society Collection.

Illustrations: Mark Coyle

Front Cover Illustration: Mark Coyle
Back Cover Photograph: Jim Theologos

International Standard Book Number: 0-87839-052-9

All rights reserved. Printed in the United States of America by Park Press, Inc., Waite Park, Minnesota.

Book Design: Corinne A. Dwyer

Published by:
    North Star Press of St. Cloud, Inc.
    P.O. Box 451
    St. Cloud, MN 56302

Dedication &
Acknowledgments

This story of four years of my childhood is as truthful as I can make it. In a very few instances I have resorted to literary license: I have taken unimportant liberties with dates, and—more significantly—I have changed several names to avoid the possibility of hurting someone. A few facts I may have wrong; my siblings have caught other mistakes in time.

To them, and to our Mother, I owe a great debt of gratitude for help and understanding. They have read the story; where they disagree on interpretation, they say, "It's your book." I only wish Father had lived long enough to tell me things only he would know.

Friends have been generous with encouragement and suggestions. Among them are Robert Harlow, Rod Hughes, Karen Johnson, and especially Peg Colegrove. Peg insisted that the book must be a memoir rather than a novel, and thus helped me find my way when I was floundering. I dedicate this book to her wisdom and friendship.

She shares the dedication with a Hiltunen child who was born after the story ends—sister Betty, whose help with my children during my early decades as a writer I hereby acknowledge with tremendous gratitude.

Rita Dwyer and Corinne Dwyer of North Star Press have my sincere gratitude and admiration for their competence and cooperation. I also thank Aili Jarvenpa, one of their authors, for her enthusiasm about the memoir, which recalls much of her own childhood, and for suggesting that I submit the manuscript to them.

My husband, John, and my children and grandchildren have read chapters over the years and kept me working when my own enthusiasm flagged. To them, love and gratitude.

There would, of course, be no story without the Hiltunen and Lempia clans, and I thank my aunts and uncles for their contributions. And the story might never have been written—in fact, I might not have become a writer at all—except for the excellent teachers who helped and encouraged me over the years.

Certainly I would never have attempted this book—so different from my earlier books (though it, too, is a form of social anthropology)—were I not so proud of my Finnish heritage and so conscious of the opportunities that "America" offered my immigrant forebears. With my first words, I demanded a lot of life, and thanks to all this help, and good fortune, and perhaps some *sisu*, "Helmi Mavis: A Finnish-American Old Age" is turning out to be as rewarding as my youth.

My parents on their wedding day, November 9, 1912. Father was twenty-seven, Mother eighteen years old.

Contents

Introduction

I was born in a small immigrant farm community in north-eastern Minnesota. After four boys, Mother hoped for a girl, and chose the name "Mavis" from a story in *Woman's World* magazine, and my middle name, Helmi, after one of her four sisters. But "Helmi" is pronounced so badly in English that, following Aunt Pearl's example, I signed all school papers Mavis Pearl Hiltunen.

When I was eighteen I needed a birth certificate and drove to the town clerk's house. Holger pointed to a line in the faded ledger and laughed. "Only a Helmi Hiltunen was born on July 27, 1919." Sure enough, there it was, in Father's flowing script. On the four-mile trip to register my birth he had forgotten the "weird" name Mother had chosen.

That split-level name may symbolize my life. On the one hand, I absorbed the difficult language, the songs, food, customs, traditions, and values of an Old World culture—and I treasure them now more than ever. On the other, I was eager to be a good American, for early in the century the pressure for "Americanization" was very strong, particularly in school. I am Finnish Helmi and American Mavis.

And my sense of identity is not at all confused. On the contrary, it is richer because I can travel, both in thought and in person, as comfortably between the two cultures as the two countries, visit happily with friends and relatives in either world, and feel proud of both.

Like all societies, Americans and Finns share basic national values among themselves. Perhaps these values are especially strong and clear among the more homogeneous Finns. But this homogeneity can be exaggerated. Even as a child, I became increasingly aware that in our small community—and more painfully, in our own family—there were sharp differences and conflicts. Some were relatively unimportant—just a matter of individual freedom, something which the Finns, after centuries of oppression, believed in so strongly, the tolerance of divisions that did not really divide the community in any fundamental sense. These differences were smoothed over by all they had in common, especially as a foreign enclave in a new country. The freedom to differ was symbolized by a little wooden plaque, from which hung a miniature rag rug and a bag of salt, still found in many Finnish homes. The words, *"Oma tupa, oma lupa,"* were burned into the wood—"In my own house I may do as I please."

By the early 1930s, however, differences split the community as they split the larger Finnish immigrant group of the country. As a child, I was aware of this mostly because of dissension within my family, among my friends, and in the community, even in the cooperative movement of which we were so very proud.

By the time I was born, the first hard years of pioneering were over. Sixty years ago smoke poured from the chimneys of our house and sauna the year around. Half a dozen cows, several calves, and a few sheep shared the barn. Chickens cackled in the coop. A team of horses neighed and stamped in the stable. Cars and snowplows and schoolbuses came and went along the roads, sleighs and wagons over the fields.

Now, nearing the end of my seventh decade of life, I am writing this memoir for several reasons. My mother, relatives, and children want me to. My grandchildren say their contemporaries will learn a lot from it, and my own contemporaries will laugh and weep over memories so much like their own. But also, it helps me find out who Helmi Mavis is, and how she grew to be me—a Finnish-American, proud of both heritages.

I begin this story at a time when I was an eight-year-old Finnish American eager to be "Americanized"—the night my youngest brother was born.

Saturday Night Sauna

Father took Mabel and me to sauna the Saturday night Bob was born. I remember Father was feeling jolly. He sang a *hulivili* song as he carried Mabel toward the log cabin beside the snow-covered brook. The kerosene lantern's yellow light danced along the frozen path. I listened to Father's song, concentrating on following the bumpy footprints without slipping, and clutched our fresh white towels. I wondered why Mother was in bed and couldn't take us to sauna as usual.

The dressing room was cold—the fire had gone out in the little cast-iron stove. We undressed in a hurry. Father helped us unbutton our garter vests and pull off our thick black woolen stockings. When Mabel shivered and pouted he tickled her and helped her hurry out of her long underwear.

The sauna was dim and mysterious in the lantern light that shone through the small dressing room window. All three benches were smooth and white from years of soap and water and the cavorting of naked bodies. We clambered up to the top bench, our feet on the middle one. The dry heat smoothed away our goose pimples.

Father came in with a towel wrapped around his waist.

The old sauna, pictured here in 1962, but essentially the same.

He dipped a pail into the galvanized iron tub full of cold water and threw some on the hot round rocks of the *kiuas*. A loud hiss, and a cloud of steam rose and spread, then vanished into the hot dry pine walls. Now it was much too hot on the top bench. We squealed and climbed down, and covered our faces with cool wet washcloths so we could breathe more easily.

Father laughed. "Wait a minute, my golden ones," he said in Finnish, "and it will be just right. The top bench is really for men."

As the steam cleared, I peeked at Father. We had never been alone with him in sauna since I could remember. He was very white right up to his neck; only his hands and head were bronzed by sun and wind. When Mother took us to sauna, we hardly paid attention to her familiar fat pink and white body and her brown arms. We often went to sauna in groups of women and girls, and if anyone was shy about it she pretended not to be. Tonight, though, there was no one but Father to give us our weekly bath.

He had to think about the routine. The boys were grown up enough by now to take care of themselves. He began to soap our backs, then decided he should first get our blood circulating with a *vihta*. He took one of the bundles of swamp cedar branches from the wooden bucket by the fire, laid it on the *kiuas* to warm it, and gently slapped our feet, legs, and backs.

"I've been a good girl, Daddy," joked Mabel. "Don't spank me any more. It's so hot."

Father pretended to be very annoyed. " 'Daddy!' 'Daddy!' I'm your *isä*. If you talk English all the time you'll forget you're a Finn. Find that soap; it must have slipped under the bench."

He lathered us with the pine tar soap and its fragrance mingled with wood smoke and cedar. He teased Mabel about her long back like a wolf's. As I soaped my short legs, I thought resentfully that it was unfair to be two years and four months older than Mabel and not an inch taller. Even Mother said that Mabel grew like a bad weed in a garden and I grew like a cow's tail. Perhaps Father was right; I stayed indoors with a book too much. Mabel was outdoors every chance she got. She even picked rocks from the fields and loaded them into a sledge with Father. Maybe I should do that too. Or maybe next summer, when I was nine, I'd start to grow.

I felt happier when Father soaped my back and sang a song about dancing the polka on a Saturday night, making up verses about me, and how *Meivessi* whirled and jumped around the floor. Only when he spoke English did he call me Mavis.

"Now shut your eyes tight." He poured pailful after pailful of warm soft spring water over our heads. When he decided the soap was all rinsed off, he doused each of us with a pailful of cold water and shooed us into the dressing room. We heard him throw water on the rocks for his own hot sauna while we were putting on our clean new flannel nightgowns.

We draped towels over our tangled hair and coats over our shoulders, and let the buckles of our arctics flap loose while we ran up the path to the lamplit house. Despite the cold—Father guessed it was 20 below—our sauna glow made the air feel warmer and softer than before.

In the kitchen my worry returned. Mother wasn't there to comb out the snarls in our damp blonde hair and tie strips of cotton rags around the strands to curl it for Sunday. She was usually bustling around the kitchen getting our supper about this time. But she was still in bed in the other room. Father was clumsy with snarls and knew nothing about curls.

Ray cranked the big wooden wall phone, one long, four short—Simonsons' number. As he waited for an answer, he read off the date from the 1928 Co-op calendar on the wall. "Hey, it's February 22—Washington's birthday." He asked for old Mrs. Simonson and told her Father would be over to get her in a few minutes.

Everything felt strange that night. When I asked what was happening, I was dismissed with a quick joke and a promise that I'd find out when the time came, so I just waited and listened, and tried to piece things together from what the grownups had said.

Supper tasted funny. Ray dished out bowls of potato soup that was slightly burned because he had forgotten to keep stirring it, and cut up some spicy salami to go with Mother's homemade rye bread. Otherwise it was an ordinary Saturday night supper, simple and quick because Saturday was the day Mother went to town to sell butter and cream and eggs. But today Father and Ray had gone instead. Now that he was thirteen, Ray was learning to drive our 1926 Model T touring car.

"Gur-ruls!" Mother called. It was strange to see her in bed before we were. She was usually the last one in bed, especially on Saturday night, when she scrubbed the kitchen floor on her hands and knees, no matter how late it was, and baked a cake for Sunday. Now we stood uncomfortably at the foot of the bed.

"Come right here, girls," she beckoned. "I want a sauna kiss. Mmm, your cheeks are like warm red apples. Give me a bite." Her smile suddenly faded and she said, "Now hurry up to bed. Maybe there will be a surprise for you in the morning if you go right to sleep."

Ray insisted we go to bed in the boys' room above the kitchen, not in our own room above Mother's and Father's bedroom. I puckered up my nose at the sharp urine smell of weasel and mink and muskrat skins stretched on boards all around the room.

But sleep comes easily after a good sauna. The quilt was wool batting tacked with yarn to blue-flowered calico, and the flannel sheets were soft. Our new nightgowns were as caressing as the water in Grandpa's lake on a summer day. We had hardly wriggled into comfortable positions, bumped bottoms ritually, and giggled once or twice before we were asleep.

It was still dark when Ray woke us up and whispered, "Come downstairs, girls. We've got company." He led the way holding a kerosene lamp.

Father grinned at us from the rocking chair. "Go see what Mother has for you."

Mother held a wrapped bundle. We could see only a small wrinkled face scrunched up with tight-shut eyes. "Here's your new little brother, girls," she said, smiling. "What shall we call him?"

"It's Washington's birthday, so of course he has to be George," Ray said.

"How did he get here?" I wondered.

"Mrs. Simonson brought him," Mother said, and quickly added, "I was thinking of Robert, but we can decide tomorrow. Now stop peeking at him. He's tired and so am I, and you can see him in the morning."

On our way back to bed—to our own room this time—we went through the kitchen and saw old Mrs. Simonson stuffing crumpled newspapers into the stove and bundling stained sheets into a basket on the porch. But I hardly noticed their rich, ripe smell, alien to the usual kitchen odors, as I hurried barefoot up the stairs. The baby's mewing cries and Mother's soft murmurs drifted up through the hot air register in the floor of our room, but couldn't keep us awake for long.

Mabel, Ray, Bob, Mother and Mavis several months after Bobby's birth.

The Maid

Mother always made Sundays special. In my memory the sun always shone on Sunday, the house was bright and clean, we wore our second-best if not our best clothes, and there were especially good things to eat. We were very likely to have visitors around coffee time, and Mother always baked what she called coffee bread—which included cookies and cakes as well as the frosted egg bread flavored with cardamom that she called *pullaa* or biscuit (*piskettiä* in Finglish)—and stored it in the pantry under the stairs.

The day after Bobby was born was special too, but it was different.

When I woke up that Sunday morning, the sun was bright on the snow and made white ripples on the ceiling. Fantasy ice ferns covered the window with thick curls. Jack Frost had been busy during the night.

I scratched a hole in the frost so I could see the snow-laden pines outside. Then I remembered the new baby and listened at the register. I heard Mother's soft voice cooing like a springtime bird in its nest, and wet sucking sounds.

I pulled gently at Mabel's hair and whispered, "Come on,

6

Mabel, let's go see the baby." For once she jumped up quickly, and we ran through the boys' room and down the stairs. Ray was in the chilly kitchen shaking up the fire in the big black cast-iron range.

Mother smiled. "My, you're up early for a Sunday. Bobby's having his first good breakfast."

Bobby's curling fingers clutched Mother's soft blue-veined breast, and milk trickled down his chin. His greedy sucking stopped and his small red head, the hair drier now, fell slowly to one side. His snuffles at the nipple turned to gentle snores.

I hesitated to ask Mother anything about her body, because she hardly ever gave me a satisfying answer. Mabel was bolder. "Mother, he sucks milk from you!"

Mother laughed. "All mothers feed babies from their own bodies, just like our cows feed their calves." She changed the subject. "You girls get dressed now. It'll be a busy day and I'm afraid the house will be full of people."

"Aren't you going to get up?"

"I've got to rest a few days so I'll have plenty of milk for the baby."

"Where's Father?"

"He's gone to get Aino Rantanen to work for a week or two. The only way I get to have a maid is to have a baby." She laughed again; her blue eyes shone with happiness. "Ray's making pancakes for breakfast. Run along now."

Mother was right. We had a house full of helpers and company that day. Miina Anderson, who was four feet, eleven inches, skinny and wrinkled, but strong and hard working, came across the hay meadow and brook to milk the cows. Uncle Ray, who lived with us while he helped Father make box bolts for the Tower box factory, fed and watered the horses. Our eleven-year-old brother Leo came home from Andersons, where he had spent the night, and said, "Holy cow! What a tiny baby!"

Ray's pancakes were so thin and dry that even blueberry sauce didn't help much, and I wished that Victor, our oldest brother, were home to cook. He worked for room and board in a hotel-restaurant in Tower, seven miles away, so he could attend high school.

But suddenly there he was. I happened to look down the road and I saw him shut the far gate and stride over the little hill to the near gate. Leo ran to open it for him, shouting, "*Vikki! Vikki! Aiti* has calved," in Finnish.

Vic was ruddy and blond. He entered laughing and stamping the snow off his boots.

"How come you're not working at the restaurant?" asked Ray.

"When Mrs. Franson heard about the baby she said she'd do it."

I reached up for a hug and kiss. I loved Vic. He was so bright he could figure out anything. He could make toy airplanes and boats that ran on rubber bands, bake cakes, invent ways to fix broken machines when there were no spare parts. He knew a lot because he read every chance he got. And he talked to me and answered my questions; he said it was okay for me to read a lot even if Father thought it would ruin my eyes.

Mother smiled at him warmly. "Oh, Victor, I'm so glad you came."

"Hello, Maw," he said in his hearty voice. "Whatcha got there? Am I s'posed to congratulate you?" He lifted the baby from her side, and said, "Good thing you like babies. They sure are homely at first."

Mother watched anxiously, then relaxed. He knew how to support the baby's head and back. He looked seriously into the little face and said, "Hey, hey, baby *poika*. What's his name? Hello, Bobby, welcome to this wonderful, terrible world."

"It's pretty wonderful today," said Mother, "but I'm glad you're here to help. Will you finish making pancakes? I don't think Ray really knows how."

When a teaspoonful of water sputtered and danced on the long black griddle that covered two stove lids, Vic spooned out batter, then flipped the pancakes expertly. Just as we finished eating, Father's Ford turned into the road, and soon he came in with the hired girl.

Aino was nothing like my notion of a maid. She looked like many other teen-aged girls: marcelled hair, orange-red lipstick applied like Clara Bow's, high-heeled shoes, and silk stockings. She stood by the door waiting to be told what to do, and Mabel took her cardboard suitcase. "Come on, I'll show you our room. Mother says you're going to sleep with us."

I went to Mother's bed and whispered, "I think she must be a flapper. She doesn't look like a maid at all." I'd seen drawings of the French Maid in the Teeny Weeny books. She wore a black dress and a frilled white apron and cap, and served things on trays.

"Oh, Mavis, she's just a farm girl like you. But I'm not sure she knows how to wash dishes in a sanitary way. You show her so she won't just give them a lick and a promise."

Aino came downstairs. She had changed to oxfords and put one of Mother's big cotton print aprons over her red rayon dress. When she started to dump dishes into the dishpan, I elbowed in and showed her our routine, with lots of boiling water and clean dishtowels. She was annoyed that a smart-aleck eight-year-old was bossing her around.

"Yeah, I heard you think you're smart. Cripes, I could tell you lots of things you don't know." She lifted her chin proudly. "I went to Pike Hall last night and danced every dance." She smiled with pleasure at my wide-eyed envy. "Three guys asked to take me home, but I knew what they were after, so I went home with my brother."

Before I could ask her what they were after, Uncle Ray came in with Aunt Hilma. He had borrowed the car to fetch her from Virginia, twenty miles away, where she went to high school. Laughing and stamping their feet, they shed their coats and hats and rubbed their hands together over the stove so they wouldn't take cold air into the bedroom.

Hilma's much prettier than Aino, I thought. She knows how to fix her shingle and make spit curls on her cheeks like the flappers in the magazines, and her mouth is really like Clara Bow's without smearing lipstick all around it. Her legs are nicer too. I looked down at my own sturdy legs and hoped some day they would be long and slim like Hilma's, and my hair would be reddish brown instead of a darkening blonde.

"Stop dreaming, kiddo," Hilma said, "and put water on to heat. I'm going to give Bobby his first bath."

Aunt Hilma and Uncle Ray went in to see their oldest sister, who held her sixth child in the crook of her arm and looked as radiant as the bright auburn hair spread out on the pillow.

"Hello, Sophie," they greeted her. Sophie was the more Americanized of her two names, Hilja Sofia. Hilja doesn't sound nearly as pleasing in English as in Finnish, with its flat "l." My own middle name was Helmi, but I didn't like it for the same reason, and I thought of myself as "Mavis Pearl Hiltunen."

Like the Finnish language, Finnish names are in a class by themselves. I loved to hear Father call Mother "Hilja" when he was feeling affectionate. It means tranquil or quiet. It was quite different from his demand for silence when we kids made a racket. *"Hiljaa!"* he would shout. or *"Ole hiljaa"* to a whining child.

Bobby was a completely American name, Finnicised only by pronouncing it "Paapi" with the "p" that is softened almost to a "b" in a language without a "b." Brother Ray was named Reino like our uncle, but we called them both Ray.

Now Uncle Ray pronounced judgment on his new nephew with a mischievous grin. "What an ugly monkey!"

Mother retorted, "You didn't look any better when you were a day old." She told Hilma what clothes to get out for the baby and just how to go about bathing him. Mabel and I watched, dumb with wonder, especially when the flannel band around his bulging tummy came off and revealed the stump that stuck out from his belly, with a string tied tightly around it.

"What's that?" I demanded to know. Hilma poked me in the tummy. "That's his *napa*. Everybody's got one." Before I had time to ponder this typically unsatisfactory grownup answer, she was washing him gently and warning us about the soft spot on his head. She laughed as a fountain of pee squirted into her face. "I'll get even when you're bigger, you *paskahousu*."

Mabel and I gasped and covered a giggle. Mother didn't let us say words like "shitpants," but Hilma got away with a lot. She was, after all, the baby sister who had been only eight months old when our grandmother died of a ruptured appendix one cold January day, and she was so pretty and good natured that Mother shrugged off her peccadilloes. Like the time she got so tired of hearing me recite, "Twinkle, twinkle, little star," that she taught me to shimmy and sing:

> Roll 'em, girls, roll 'em,
> Everybody roll 'em,
> Roll 'em down and show your pretty knees.

Hilma took the bundle smelling of Johnson's Baby Powder into the kitchen and stood before Father, who was reading the *Duluth Herald* in the rocking chair. "Here, Pete, take your baby and let Sophie sleep."

Father's crooked grin appeared as he settled the baby in his arms, touched his cheek tenderly, and said, "You're the refuge of my old age. You're the caboose."

"Huh!" snorted Hilma. "You've said that for at least two babies. How many cabooses do you think a train has? Maybe you'd better sleep in the sauna from now on."

Father ignored her and crooned a Finnish lullaby as he rocked. It was a nonsense song about a mouse skiing on a road, pulling a little sled.

> Where are you going, dear mouse?
> Beyond the bay and up to the moon;
> Beyond Kiirola, up into a tree.
> Where were you on Sunday?
> Herding the pastor's cows.
> What did you get for pay?
> Five, six little boys.
> What were their names?
> Iitami, Aatami, the shoemaker of Pitchpoint,
> Make me some black shoes, tippity-tappity ones,
> So I can get married.
> Where from far beyond the pastures will you find a bride?
> From among the girls of Piinopirkko,
> Who are so heavy that horses cannot haul them,
> *Paju luokat lonkotellen*
> *Rauta kiskot kinkotellen.*

Father let me take the sleeping baby back to Mother. Hilma watched to see that I didn't let his head wobble.

"What time is it?" Mother asked drowsily. "I bet you all forgot about Peter's coffee and it's almost dinner time. Good thing I made a big pot of venison stew yesterday when I knew the baby was coming. It's in the porch, probably frozen. Have the girls make Jello for dessert. And there's a marble cake for coffee on top of my wardrobe. That's one place the boys wouldn't think of looking."

Hilma took over in the kitchen. "Aino, put the stew on to heat. Mavis, you know how to make Jello; cool it out in the snow until it's nearly set, then bring it into the porch. Mabel, we don't need a special tablecloth today; there'll be plenty of things to wash now. Just give the oilcloth a good cleaning and show Aino where the dishes and stuff are and help her set the table. I'll cut the bread. Oh, for crying out loud, here comes Pa, driving the old sleigh."

The heavy door opened again, and Grandpa came in like an elf on the cold blast. He wasn't much bigger than I was—a little over five feet tall. His eyes were teary from the cold and his mustache was frosted with miniature icicles.

We abandoned our chores long enough to hug him and get a mustache kiss and a bristly chin rub. He chortled and tickled us, and hefted us to see how we had grown in the past week.

While he took off his sheepskin coat and its matching hat with earflaps that tied under his chin, he said, "I had to wait at Wahlsten's Station for 65 iron ore cars to go by. On Sunday! The mines sure are busy." Then Mabel and I each took him by a gnarled hand and led him into the bedroom to show off the baby.

"*No niin, Hiljakulta*. So all went well this time?" It was clear that she really was his *kulta*, his golden one, his darling.

Hilma called us back to our chores. We pulled the table away from the window, extended its drop leaves, and crowded ten plates around it. Father didn't usually allow casual conversation at mealtimes. Food was hard won and eating was serious business. We had to eat all the food we took from the bowls and platters passed around the table.

Today the mood was much more relaxed. To ordinary requests like "Please pass the butter," and "Are there any more bread-and-butter pickles? You're nearest the pantry, Mabel," we added remarks about the baby. "Who does he look like, do you think?" "Can't tell till he opens his eyes." "Do you like the name Bobby?"

Father took his usual Sunday nap on the brown leather sofa in the bedroom. This was a signal for quiet, and, dishes done, we went upstairs with Aino. We investigated her Tangee lipstick, the curling iron she heated over a kerosene lamp, the face powder in the box decorated with soft powder puffs, and the Hind's Honey and Almond Cream she rubbed on her hands. She was more interested in Uncle Ray. How old was he? Did he have a girl? Did he go to dances? She'd never seen him at Pike Hall.

We settled down to read. I didn't even glance at *Little Women*, which I had taken out of the school library for the third time. Nor did I raid the boys' room for *Whiz Bang*, with its puzzling, and obviously dirty jokes, nor for the scary detective magazines with their photos of murder scenes marked with heavy Xs where the body was found and lines of heavy dots and arrows which showed how the murderer probably came and went. No. Aino's little suitcase held greater treasures—copies of *True Confessions* and *Love Story* magazine. Forbidden fruit that I dared savor only away from Mother, and consequently more appealing than any other reading. I leafed through one and looked at the photos of couples embracing, gazing at each other adoringly, or quarreling and weeping. Then I settled on a story.

He was gone—her handsome prince with his dark pomaded hair, his deep, thrilling voice, and smoldering eyes, and his long, sleek car. As she crushed the fatal letter in her trembling hands, suddenly the room reeled round her.

When she opened her eyes again, her mother was anxiously kneeling beside her, cradling her head tenderly, offering her a glass of water.

"Oh, my dear daughter! Did you forget all my wise counsel and let him have his way?"

The two women, heart-broken gray-haired mother and lovely wayward daughter, fell into each other's arms and sobbed their hearts out.

I was startled when Hilma came and snatched the magazine away. "Oh, Mavis, you're too young to read such trash."

"But you read it, and so does Aunt Lydia, and the Juntunen girls have piles of them," I pouted.

"You know your Mother doesn't like them, and anyhow, it's coffee time and Grandpa and I have to leave right after."

We went downstairs willingly to set the table. Unlike regular meals, Sunday afternoon coffee was a time for talk and jokes. For arguing politics, from who should be the next president to the even more important choice of a county road commissioner—because if our friend Jacob Pete got in, there would surely be a road job for Father. For gossip and discussion of community affairs: the last Farmer's Club meeting and the next; whom to name as manager of the new consumers' co-operative general store—"the Kwap"—four miles away. The rural phone company's problems.

And any number of interesting things I could hear about only if I sat quietly on the stairs or on "The Little Floor." As I passed that hideaway—a piece of the second floor that stuck out past the wall of the boys' room almost to the stair railing—I piled all the magazines to one side in case I wanted to sit there and eavesdrop later, or read if I got bored with the conversation.

Coffee Time

Aunt Hilma had set the table with cake, cookies, and *pullaa*, and thick cream and sugar. The aroma of freshly ground and newly brewed coffee pervaded the kitchen. I took Mother a cup of coffee and a slice of whole wheat bread spread with butter and rhubarb jam. We heard the door bang again, and Matt Mattson's beery voice saying, "*Hyvää päivää.*"

Finnish men are not boisterous greeters. Even Father, who was usually talkative in public, would arrive at the Co-op, note the presence of two or three neighbors, nod slightly, make his purchases, and then say "*No niin,*" as a preliminary to remarks about the haying, the prospects for a Finnish county road commissioner, the weather. . . . Now he noncommittally returned Matt's courtesy, saying, "*Päivää.*"

I knew why Mother made a face when she heard Matt's voice. He lived in a dark and dirty little log cabin in the woods near by, and plied his visitors with home brew. He had been a bartender in Tower before Prohibition. Many of his guests were young boys like Victor, whom he taught card games. And his slovenly ways evoked a "*hyi, hyi*" of disgust from Mother, who, though she fought a losing battle to keep our little house tidy,

**Grandpa Lempia,
1944.**

was a fanatic scrubber.

I hurried into the kitchen, got the spittoon for the squirts of juice from Matt's constant chewing of "snoose"—Copenhagen snuff—and set it carefully beside his boots, which dripped melting snow on the rag rug. Though Mother thought he was a bad influence on the boys, and I sometimes took Father to task for having insisted that he be my godfather, I rather liked him. I loved to dance, and I overlooked his faults because he cheerfully played the accordion at dances and parties at Vermillion Hall, and rarely went anywhere on skis or bike without his *hanuri* in the packsack strapped to his back.

Despite his pungent odor, he didn't look at all evil or sinister as he sat smiling in his favorite chair beside the door, round faced and ruddy, his dark woolen pants held up over his paunch by thick grimy striped suspenders, his heavy woolen shirt stained with the traces of many meals. He puffed out his cheeks, popped his bloodshot eyes, and loudly cracked his knuckles to make me laugh.

"Come to coffee," Hilma invited. Mabel and I weren't allowed to drink coffee; Father said it would ruin our complexions. We filled small plates with goodies but left the table to the grown-ups. I took the rocking chair before Mabel reached it, and she sat on the bottom stair. I watched Matt and Grandpa put a lump of sugar between their front teeth, pour coffee into their saucers, and sip it through the sugar. Many old Finns did that, but I wished my Grandpa wouldn't. It looked old-fashioned and not "Americanized," which was Mother's standard of proper manners.

But Grandpa was so dear. He chortled and twinkled as he talked. "What are you learning in that Tower school, *Vikki*?" he asked after his first happy slurp of coffee.

Vic glanced at Father, who was gazing down the snowy road, and said, "Oh . . . well, I like Algebra, because I need math to be an engineer, and my English teacher's good, and History's interesting, though a lot of it's bunk, as Henry Ford says."

Uncle Ray put his cup down. Like Vic, he spoke Finnish fluently. "You know, it's funny, since I graduated from Duluth High School last year, I've forgotten all that stuff. And here I am working in the woods and waiting to be called to a job in the Soudan mine, just as if I'd never even finished eighth grade."

Father didn't think it was funny. "That's what I tell *Vikki*. He's learning a lot of useless junk when he should be peeling jackpines and helping me feed this *porukka*."

Father's voice was low and reasonable enough, but his words made Vic's face turn red and his eyes mist with anger behind his round steel-rimmed glasses. I saw that he was trying to control his temper, as quick and hot as Father's. But his voice rose. "I *have* to study all that if I want to graduate and get anywhere."

Matt looked around the table, bent over his coffee again and silently concentrated on the good food he was always sure of at the Hiltunen farm. Grandpa tried to restore the happy Sunday atmosphere with a joke. He chuckled and smiled and exuded good will as he said, "That's what I tell Hilma. Why is she studying so hard? She'll just get married and wash diapers."

Then he saw that he had made things worse. Victor and Father were both on the point of angry speech when Uncle Ray broke in to smooth things over. His low, serious voice commanded attention.

"Well, even if I forget a lot, I sure am glad I got a diploma, because I can read and understand a lot of things that would have been Greek to me if I'd only gone through eighth grade. Anyway, you know Finns have always believed in education. *Isä*, you told me that Finns weren't even allowed to get married if they couldn't read."

I reached between Matt and Victor for another sour cream cookie and retreated to the rocker to listen as Grandpa replied. "That was really a church rule. The Lutheran *pappis* wanted everyone to read the Bible, and kids didn't have many rights until they were confirmed at age fourteen." He paused and looked around as if he had just realized that most of us didn't know much about the Old Country, and it was his duty, as the patriarch of the clan, to enlighten us.

"Learning to read was one way we could stay Finns when we were under the thumb of Sweden all those years, and then under Russia. Just before 1900 the Czar sent over that *Poperikoffi* to rule over the Grand Duchy of Finland, and he was a bad one, a real dictator. He wanted to turn all the Finns into Russians."

"But you came here in about 1885—that was before Bobrikov," Uncle Ray remembered.

"*Joo.* I came because there wasn't much work to be had in Finland, and *meikäläiset* had to live on herring and skim milk. The little farms couldn't be divided among all the kids people had in those days. . ."

Aunt Hilma snorted with laughter. "Hah! you should talk, with eight—and Pete with six already."

"True enough, Hilma," Grandpa said. "Anyway, we were very poor. My father was a woodcarver in Vaasa on the Gulf of Bothnia. One year everything froze and the herring didn't come in, and we were hungry. The big lumber and mining companies and railroad builders in *Ameriika* needed workers, and with the steamship companies, they made it easy for Finns to cross the Big Puddle."

I looked at my cookie. Half of it was left, but my appetite was gone—something Ray teased would never happen to me unless I was dying. But Grandpa went on with his story as if it had been a great adventure to be young and hungry and leaving home forever.

"Father went to *Ameriika* first. Then I crossed to Sweden and to Liverpool and took a ship to *Ameriika*, two years later. But I was only 15 and couldn't get a passport, so I stowed away until we were halfway across the ocean. And when I landed in *Ameriika*, the officials kept writing down that I was Russian. I said, "No! FINN! FINN!' "

Father liked to tell his story too. "They tried to do the same to me when I came in 1907. *Poperikoffi* had been assassinated and there was a little more freedom, but for many years the rul-

ers tried to make us speak Russian and become Orthodox Catholics, and conscript us into the army, and young people kept crossing the Big Puddle until war broke out in 1914."

Ray asked, "How come the Russians let you go?"

"It was easy enough to get forged papers and passports,"
Father explained. "Tickets were cheap, and those who had already got jobs in *Ameriika* sent passports and tickets to their
relatives and *omanpaikkasia*. The Lutheran *pappis* helped us
get to the ports. They didn't want us turned into Catholics. Some
of them left too."

Aino put another plate of *pullaa* on the table, and while
the men helped themselves I saw my chance to ask a question.
"Father, you're always talking about *omanpaikkasia*, like Matt
Holappa and Heikki Hiltula. Does that mean other Finlanders?"

Father buttered a slice of *pullaa* while he replied. "No.
People from the same parish or neighborhood. Holapan Matti
was our neighbor in Sanginkylä, Utajärvi, Oululääni"— he liked
to roll out the syllables of his home place names slowly and rhythmically—"well, he came first, right here to Minnesota, and when
he had saved a little money, he sent me his passport and a ticket.
I landed in Portland, Maine, and came to Tower by train. After
I saw that there were so many Finns and so much work to be
had, and had earned enough money, I sent tickets to brother
Arvid and our neighbor Heikki. Vermilion is full of my *omanpaikkasia*."

"That's the wooden suitcase you came with, up in the pantry in our room," Ray commented.

"It's still there, is it?" Father was pleased. "I suppose the
mice have made their nests in it by now."

Uncle Ray could imagine a young man's feelings about
leaving home for a new land. "Did you plan to stay or to go back
some day?"

"I think some of us really believed we'd make a fortune
and go back and live like *herras*," said Father. "I thought I'd go
into some business; I've always liked selling. I wanted to go to
Valparaiso College in Indiana and study business after I had
earned a little money in lumber camps and road work. But then
I got married, and here I am picking rocks out of the fields so I
can farm and feed five kids."

"Six!"

He looked around and grinned at the young ones who had
corrected him. The grin faded as Vic challenged him. "If you

wanted to study, why didn't you go to Duluth? That's much nearer, and there's a Work People's College there."

"Too Red for me," Father mildly replied. Again he looked down the road. He drummed the fingers of his right hand on the table, tapping first with his little finger, finally with his thumb, over and over again. He often did this when he was thinking, or trying to keep his temper.

Grandpa was reminded of an interesting bit of news. "I read in the *Työmies* that in Russia all the peasants are getting land of their own and don't have to work for the lords anymore."

No one spoke for a moment. The air felt heavy, as before a summer storm. I left the rocker and crept quietly to the top of the stairs, where I could peer down through the railing without being part of the scene. Ray and Leo, who cared much more about skiing and trapping than politics, came past me and flopped on their beds for a nap.

Father's finger tapping slowed as he finally spoke. "*Niinkö? Vai niin?* Well, of course the *Työmies* is a *komunisti* paper and naturally it prints things like that. What it doesn't say is that *Stalini* plans to make this so-called land of their own into huge collective farms run by the government. It's not private land at all, not like our homestead land here. He's turning into a bigger tyrant than *Poperikoffi*. So they're not really farming at all and there's more hunger every year."

"That's a lot of bullshit!" Vic burst out. "You read only the capitalist papers with their anti-Soviet propaganda."

Father's temper was barely under control as he retorted, "And you spend too much time with Eino, and you know who he hangs around with—the Young Workers' League and all those *komunistit*. You'd be better off in a logging camp or an iron mine than in school if that's the kind of thing you're learning."

Now Vic was really angry. "School has nothing to do with it. Anyone can see how the rich grab and control everything." He ignored Uncle Ray's friendly signal to calm down. "You came to this country hoping to be better off. Whose fault is it that you have to pick rocks and shovel cow shit? Did the farmers cut down the tall trees that had been here for ages? No. It was the lumber barons who raped the woods and burned the slashings and burned the humus out of the soil. Is Oliver Mining Company paying its workers decent wages? No. And when they ask for more, and go on strike, they're fired and blacklisted forever. And even your bourgeois Finnish businessmen side with the big shots. But you won't read the only paper that tells the facts."

Father had sat silent during Vic's tirade, his face growing redder and redder. Now he leaned his elbows on the table and pointed a hard forefinger at his oldest son. "*Poika,* as long as you sit at my table and eat the bread I sweat for, you talk to me respectfully. I'll never allow that Red paper in this house."

I clutched the stair railing tightly and felt a lump form in my stomach. The sunny day now felt dark and threatening. The ordinary words "red" and "worker" held new and dangerous meanings, and I didn't dare ask what *komunisti* meant for fear of provoking more quarreling.

Hilma had heard Mother call and slipped away to the bedroom. Now she came back and said, "Please calm down, everybody. This is no time to fight. Sophie says it upsets her so much when she's nursing that her milk turns bad and the baby gets colic and cries a lot." She fetched the big blue enamel coffeepot and refilled cups.

The storm had passed. Uncle Ray was talking—serious, soothing, deliberate. "Anyway, Pa got our 160 acres of homestead land here with 40 years to pay, and no one tells us how to farm it or what religion to believe in or what language we have to speak." He smiled at his father. "Pa's got along all these years with about two dozen words of English." He was teasing; Grandpa's English was adequate for serving on the town board and doing business.

As he paused to finish his coffee, the wall clock struck four slow resonant notes. He pushed away his dishes, leaned his elbows on the table, and looked around at everyone. "No matter what problems we Finns have had, under Sweden or Russia or here in America, we've got *sisu.*"

I crept down the stairs to listen. *Sisu* was a magic word—something all Finns were proud of—and Uncle Ray was making everyone feel a little better. I listened carefully as he explained what he meant by *sisu.*

"We're tough; we've got guts; we keep going through thick and thin. We work like mules . . . and" (he interrupted himself and laughed) "maybe we're just as stubborn. Anyway, nothing gets us down for very long. So I guess we'll make it even if we have to pick rocks and peel pulpwood right now." He smiled at everyone, ruffled Mabel's hair, and said, "Now I guess I'll have to borrow your car, Pete, to take Hilma back to town. Maybe she'll learn to type before she has to wash diapers."

Grandpa got into his little sleigh and, reminding me of

Santa Claus, waved, called his Finnish-English (Finglish) *"Pye pye,"* clucked his tongue to the horse and was off in a spray of snow. Father banged out of the house and strapped on his skis. I knew he hoped to find a card game at Miettunens'. The tightness in my stomach and throat loosened as I watched him push back on the ski poles with long, rhythmic strokes and glide down the road.

Matt shrugged into his thick mackinaw, winked at Vic, and asked him to come over and play cards for a while. Vic blinked and smiled apologetically. "Not tonight, Matt. I better stay with *Aiti* and the kids. Maybe next time."

Mabel and I went to see Mother and the baby. Vic came in too, and said hoarsely, "I'm sorry, Maw. I know I shouldn't get so mad. Father'll get over it and everything will be okay. I'll stay tonight and see about the evening chores. I can get to town with the mailman in the morning."

Mother reached up to pat his cheek as he bent over the baby. "Thanks, Victor. God bless you. I just wish there hadn't been a fight today, when I need to rest and want to thank God for everything."

While Aino, who had watched the whole scene in fascinated silence, cleared away the coffee things, Vic assigned chores. "Hey you boys, come down from there and clean the barn and water the cows before Miina comes to milk. Girls, carry wood."

I was about to tease him for acting like *Poperikoffi* when he went on. "I'll get water, and tell you what, if you do everything fast I'll bake another cake tonight and pack your lunch pails."

Mabel and I put on our old coats, warm caps, scarves, mittens, and arctics, and pulled the heavy little sled down to the woodshed. First we hauled big birch logs for the bedroom woodbox. Then we made four trips with smaller pieces of firewood for the kitchen range. On our last trip, we dashed to the outhouse behind the barn so we wouldn't have to come out after dark. The sunset was a deep orange behind the pine trees across the meadow.

Each of us shivered on one of the holes, a couple of pages from an old Montgomery Ward catalog in our hands. "At least it doesn't smell as bad as in summer," Mabel remarked.

"No, but it's too cold to sit here and read old papers and magazines. Wonder why the corset ads last the longest? No one wants to use them." I felt better as I giggled with my sister.

While Leo fed and watered the horses, the other boys took care of the milk. Little Mrs. Anderson carried in two huge pails

brimming with warm foaming milk, and got the morning milk from the cool pantry. Vic poured it, pailful by pailful, into the bulging silver bowl atop the separator. Ray turned and turned the handle. Rich cream poured out of one spout and white skim milk out of the other into separate five-gallon cans. A loud "ding" punctuated each whirring turn of the handle. I made up one of the silly ditties I liked to share with Mother:

> It may be Sunday—ding!
> And pretty special—ding!
> But chores are never end—ding!

I could daydream during some chores, but not while washing the separator. Mother was very fussy about that. Each of the 32 shallow cone-shaped discs had to be washed separately in warm soapy water that soon turned greasy from cream, then scalded in streams of boiling water from the teakettle, along with spouts, milk pails, and bowl.

After our supper of salami sandwiches and marble cake, I left "the maid" to do the dishes and went in to see the baby. Mother asked me to change his diaper. I said "Ish" out of habit, but Bobby's soiled diaper didn't turn my usually queasy stomach.

Perhaps it was because Mother said, "You were all tiny and help-less like him once, and had to be taken care of. I was too, and every-one in the whole world. This is how we all get our start. So I know you'll be my good girl and help me a lot now." I solemnly vowed I would.

Vic was alone in the kitchen, stirring cake batter. "Good-night little *sisko*," he said as I started to climb the stairs. I was sleepy, but I hoped to hear more from Aino about how it felt to be sixteen.

Then I saw my schoolbooks on the sideboard. The baby had driven arithmetic clear out of my mind. And perhaps I didn't want to remember, serious as I was about school, because I hadn't really understood Miss Nikkinen's brief explanation of long di-vision just before she dismissed us on Friday. I came back down the stairs and settled myself at the table that served for doing homework as well as meals and Father's solitary cribbage and card games.

"Oh, Victor," I wailed after a few minutes of struggling with the new kind of problem. "I'm so sleepy I can't figure this out, and Teacher will be mad at me tomorrow."

Vic popped the cake into the oven and sat down to explain the mysteries of dividends and divisors and carrying numbers. Soon all the problems were done. Father came in silently, hung his sheepskin coat and cap on the deer antlers by the stove, and disappeared into the bedroom without a word. My throat began to feel tight again.

Vic spoke softly. "Listen, don't let him bother you. Remem-ber he came from the Old Country thinking life would be a lot easier here, and he has to work very, very hard. Don't you worry about it if we argue. He makes me so mad sometimes, but he's got a lot of *sisu* and he gets things done in the community. So for-get it, little *sisko*, and just keep on studying."

Then he laughed. "Look who I'm telling to study. I never saw anyone so serious about school, not even me. When you were in first grade, Father and Mother would sit here having their morning coffee, and they knew that at 6:15 on the dot you'd be here in your nightgown, rubbing your eyes and looking at the clock to be sure you wouldn't be late for school."

That old story, I thought, annoyed. When would they all stop thinking it was so funny?

But Vic had more on his mind. "Of course school isn't every-thing, but it helps you get what you want out of life. And I know you want a lot. You said so before we knew you could talk at all. You were maybe nine months old and I was getting ready for school. You were sitting right there on the floor by the door, and you cried for the cookies you saw Mother putting in my lunch pail. Maw said, 'Oh, give her one,' and you said. . . "

I chimed in with my often-repeated first words. *"Ei kun paljo."* (No, but a lot.)

I was too sleepy to ponder why that was considered so funny. Of course I wanted a lot. Things from the Sears Roebuck catalog. A nice house like some I had seen in Ely and Virginia and Minneapolis. Trips on ocean liners like those I saw pictures of in Aunt Hilma's *Delineator* and *Cosmopolitan*. I wanted to travel and see strange places and people. And act in plays, and write stories, and be praised, and admired, and loved.

But my list was not as long and clear as usual, because right now what I wanted most of all was sleep. Everyone but Vic and me was already snoring, forcefully or gently.

I undressed, got into my new nightgown and decided it didn't matter if it was wrong side out, peed into the slop pail, covered it with newspaper, held my hand over the lamp chimney, and blew out the light.

As I wriggled under the quilt and snuggled against Mabel's chunky body, I murmured, *"Ei kun paljo."*

A blurry idea crossed my consciousness: Why hadn't I asked Vic where Bobby came from? And what a *komunisti* was? And why a red paper made Father so angry?

What I wanted most of all these days was to know things. But almost everyone else brushed off my questions. I thought vaguely of going downstairs to ask him, but the prospect of getting out of the warm bed was discouraging, and sleep overcame me before I could move a muscle.

Country School 40

I was usually eager to go to school on Mondays, and especially today, with such exciting news. We peeked at Bobby while we huddled near the hot bedroom stove and pulled on our long underwear, garter vests and hated black wool stockings with the gray feet, our flannel bloomers and petticoats, then our woolen skirts and sweaters. We begged Aino to dry her hands and brush our hair while we ate our oatmeal. Vic was gone, but sure enough, he had filled our lunch pails with venison sandwiches and orange cake, small mustard jars of cocoa and an apple apiece. It was a new week, and maybe it would be a nice one if Father had forgotten yesterday's anger. He and Uncle Ray had already left for the woods.

Ray and Leo hurried in from cleaning the barn and feeding and watering the cows, and changed their smelly rubber barn boots for laced-up lumberjack boots. I ran upstairs for my forgotten shoes.

It was almost eight o'clock, and Mr. Hujanen was already coming through the near gate, his team trotting briskly, their harness bells jingling in the crisp air. They snorted and stamped as they waited in front of the house. We were usually ready and waiting, but not today. We hurriedly pulled on arctics and coats, tassel caps and scarves and mittens, grabbed our books and lunch pails, and ran out, our coats flying open.

We climbed the two steps into the rectangular blue wooden box that served as a school bus. In winter it rested on heavy steel-clad wooden runners, in fall and spring on high wheels. A small enclosed metal stove threw off heat from a back corner. Charcoal foot warmers and blankets kept us warm.

Five children moved along the wooden benches to make room for us—shy, delicate Madie Poyhtari, who kept house for her widowed father; Vaino and Elsie Miettunen, tall, blond, high-cheekboned, and sparing with words; vivacious Elsie Anderson, who curled her dark brown hair every day and was considered boy crazy, and her blond brother Helmer, who was very shy with girls. We four Hiltunens were all talkers, and today Mabel and I were bursting with news.

There were three more stops on the two-mile stretch to school. Our nearest neighbors, Nannie and Mamie Krapu, climbed in first. We liked them because they wanted to be beauty operators and were always willing to fuss with our hair and nails. At the next stop they made room for Aili Juntunen, my best friend, and her sister Elvi, who was in eighth grade with Ray. Last came the Keinanen boys.

I blushed when curly-headed Reino sat across from me, our knees touching. We had been good friends since first grade, when Miss Odencrans paired us off in a little dance to the song:

> How'd you do, my partner,
> How'd you do today?
> Let us dance in a circle,
> I will show you the way.

But his brother Roy teased me about being fat, and said fat people died young. I was sure I wasn't really fat—not like Mother and a couple of the schoolgirls. I just thought he was mean, and maybe all redheads were.

As soon as Aili got in, Mabel and I babbled about how cute Bobby was, and how tiny, and what a surprise it had been to wake up in the night and find that Mrs. Simonson had brought him to our house.

Thirteen-year-old Nannie snorted at our ignorance. "Huh! It was no surprise to me! Your mother sure had a big belly lately."

I wriggled with embarrassment and tossed my head. I

School 40 in St. Louis County.

tucked a new idea into the back of my mind and retorted, "Oh, we knew! Mother told us a long time ago that a new brother or sister was coming." I thought back to the day when Mother had sat down heavily in the rocking chair and told Mabel and me that there would be something new in our house before long. We guessed at new curtains, then at linoleum for the kitchen floor— so that Mother wouldn't have to varnish it twice a year—before she told us about the new baby. That afternoon about fifteen women came over with presents. It was fun to feel the soft blankets, sweaters, tiny bootees, and undershirts, and then to fold them away in a drawer with several dozen flannel and birdseye diapers.

The bigger boys were poking one another and snickering. I asked Roy if he'd done his long division. As the bus turned into the school yard, two other busses full of kids came along from other roads, and the cloakrooms filled with noise and jostling as we hung up our wraps and pulled off our arctics. Because our lunches would have frozen in the cloakroom, we set our lunch pails around the big stove encased in a cylinder of shiny black embossed metal and put our jars of soup and cocoa in the warm water of the evaporating pan on top.

Teacher had the room clean and a fire going, but it was still chilly when I hurried to my seat in the fourth grade row near the door while Mabel took hers by the window with the other first graders. Miss Nikkinen rang the brass hand bell to hurry stragglers along.

We all stood up, right hands on chests where we thought our hearts must be, and recited in ragged unison with Teacher, eyes on the 48-star flag above the blackboard, "I pledge allegiance to the flag of the United States of America, and to the republic for which it stands, one nation indivisible, with liberty and justice for all."

Black profile cutouts of George Washington and Abraham Lincoln still adorned the bulletin board space above the blackboards, along with red Valentine hearts and Cupids. Soon they would be replaced by tulips and windmills and little Dutch boys and girls, and it would be warm enough to stick some on the windows, too.

This month it was Sivia Salmela's job to X out days on the calendar chalked on the front blackboard. Above, in bright blue, was printed February 1928. The 11th and 22nd were marked in red, ordinary days in white. Now Sivia was chalking out Friday, Saturday and Sunday.

Miss Nikkinen started the day's routine. "Fourth grade, if you haven't done your long division, get to work on that." I thought thankfully of Victor. "If you have, study your geography lesson. Third grade, I will test you on spelling in twenty minutes. Look at the clock now. What time is it, second grade? Open your readers to page 62 and be ready as soon as the first graders are settled."

I opened my geography book to the chapter on Egypt, but I had already read about the Pyramids and the *fellahin* and the way they drew water from the Nile for their crops. I watched while pretty Miss Nikkinen encouraged the first graders to create patterns with little tiles in various shapes of yellow, green, red, purple and orange wood, or to work gray-green globs of clay into snakes and bowls and animals.

Some of the kids were restless; they hated to stay put at a desk after the freedom of the weekend. Several of the lean, long-jawed Hujanen clan were in the lower grades; one or another was always at the pencil sharpener or wastebasket, or raising a hand for permission to go to the toilet—though if that was just an excuse to get out, I wondered how they could stand the cold outhouses. Another big family was represented by several of its pale gray-green members with their greenish-blond hair cut around a bowl, and their simple, dark clothes. They acted especially slow and sleepy today. Their parents were Holy Rollers, and maybe they had been so carried away last night that the meeting went on and on.

As the room warmed up from the fire and the twenty young bodies wriggling in their seats, the schoolroom smells grew stronger: pencil shavings, chalk dust, sweaty woolen socks, floor varnish, the hot paint near the stove, books, ink. Chalk sometimes screeched on the blackboard and made me shudder. Once in a while someone sneezed or farted or brought forth an exaggerated belch. It was a very ordinary school day.

The second graders gathered by Teacher's desk, seated on low chairs, and took turns standing up to read aloud about Grandfather Pig, who couldn't find his glasses and had the whole family scurry around looking for them until a little grandson noticed them pushed back above his forehead.

Then the third graders practiced their spelling. As Teacher flashed cards one by one, I wrote each word several times in my best penmanship. It was much more fun to try to make perfectly shaped and joined letters than to practice the boring drills of overlapping slanted lines called "Push-Pull," and the overlapping circles that were supposed to just barely touch the upper and lower lines for two spaces in our floppy Palmer Method books. I had to remind myself to hold the pen just so, not to press down so hard that I would bend the nib and have to push a shiny new one into the tapered black penholder, and not to touch the paper with hand or wrist, but rest my weight on my forearm. My right arm, of course. Mabel was already having trouble because she was left-handed and it was hard to hold the pencil in her right hand all the time.

Just as I was dipping my pen into the inkwell set in my desk, Walter Hujanen jostled my elbow and grinned toothily back at me on his way to put logs into the stove. I stifled a squeal of rage, and when Teacher looked over, I pretended nothing had happened, and quietly pressed my blotter on the splattered desk and paper. If I told on Walter I would get it at recess: "Yah, Yah, tattle tale, tattle tale, hanging on a bull's tale; When the bull pisses you'll get a nice cup of tea."

Our geography lesson was easy. Miss Nikkinen assigned

us a colored map of Egypt for next day. She turned her sweet oval face to look at the Regulator clock on the wall, with its softly swinging pendulum, and dismissed us for our fifteen-minute recess.

The boys hurried out for a snowball fight, but after a quick trip to the outhouse marked "Girls," the girls came in to play Pease Porridge Hot or sit in pairs and whisper, glancing around and giggling about their secret opinions of others.

This was my chance to tell Aili about the new baby without being teased. Aili's deep blue eyes grew round, and her sweet mouth formed "Oh"s and "Gee"s under her little snub nose while I exclaimed, "He's so cute! And so tiny! I held him already and changed his diaper, and I watched Mother feed him from her tits!" I whispered the last word very softly. "And we have a maid to do the housework while Mother rests and gets enough milk so he will grow."

Aili was a very satisfactory listener. She had been my best friend since the spring of first grade (even though I had been promoted to second grade midyear), when Mabel had swollen glands and Miss Odencrans feared an epidemic of mumps and suggested I stay with another family for a week. We exchanged confidences and giggled over anything and nothing in bed or seated on our secret mossy boulder in the woods just off the road. One silly day we lowered our bloomers and left heart-shaped imprints of our little bottoms in the damp clay of a field behind the barn.

After recess the older children were drawing winter scenes in crayon on tan construction paper passed down each row, and the first graders were gathered around Teacher reciting their phonics, "Ab eb ib ob ub, see the big tin tub. Ad ed id od ud . . ." when an upper-room girl brought Miss Nikkinen a note from the other teacher.

She stood up at her desk, patted the blonde bun at the nape of her neck, and said, "Put your work away, boys and girls. Clear your desks and sit up straight. The County Superintendent of Schools, Mr. Barnes, is visiting our school today. Tuck in your shirt, Gilbert. Comb your hair quickly, girls. When he comes in, you all stand up and say, 'Good morning, Mr. Barnes.'"

The door opened again and a gigantic figure filled the doorframe. As we slid out of our seats and stood up, we forgot our orders until Miss Nikkinen looked meaningfully at us and mouthed the words, "Good morning, Mr. Barnes."

Never had I seen such a tall man, with such a huge beak of

a nose and such a serious look. His dark suit and tie, his white shirt, and his gleaming black shoes proclaimed him a city dweller.

"Good morning, children." The deep voice matched the man. "Have you been good students?" Another meaningful glance from Teacher elicited some meek nods and yeses.

"What country do we live in?" He pointed a sausage-sized finger at Roy, who blushed as red as his hair before he stammered, "A-america."

"Well, yes. The *what* of America?"

"The U-nided States of America."

His next target was a second grader, Evelyn Dahl. "What state do we live in?"

"Minnesota."

"Very good. And what county?"

A nervous third grader answered, "P-peyla?"

"Well, yes, I'm told that's an old name for this community because early Italian settlers named Peyla handled the mail. But now it's Vermilion Township in Saint . . ."

As he waited, I filled in just loudly enough to be heard, "Saint Louis County."

"Very good! And this is School Number Forty of Saint Louis County, Minnesota, The United States of America. It's the best country in the world, with liberty and justice for all. I'm sure you say that every morning when you pledge allegiance. Now, who can tell me the name of our national anthem? No one? Remember, all the school children in the country were asked to vote on it not long ago."

Mabel spoke up clearly. "The Star Spangled Banner."

"Excellent! Remember it's the land of the free and the home of the brave. And that if you work hard and save your pennies, you can succeed in life and be anything you want to be. You boys might even get to be President. Study hard now. Well!" He rubbed his huge hands together. "Now I think you all deserve a lollipop." A smile lit his craggy face as he strode out of the room with Teacher.

Heads turned to me, the bookworm who knew so many words. "What's a lollipop?"

"It's a chocolate-covered caramel candy on a stick," I replied confidently.

When the awesome personage handed out ordinary all-day suckers in rainbow colors like the first graders' tiles, I blushed with embarrassment. But no one made fun of me for exaggerating the glamour of the unexpected treat.

Teacher didn't find it easy to restore routine. She glanced at the clock and said, "All right, children, we'll begin our lunch hour a little bit early today, but save your lollipops for dessert. Next time a man visits us, though, please remember to say 'Yes, sir' and 'No, sir.' I'm glad you remembered to say 'Thank you' at least."

We had another lesson in good manners that day. When Miss Nikkinen came in from the teachers' little apartment after lunch, she carried something I recognized. For weeks I had worked hard making an art notebook for the county fair. Teacher had given me small prints of famous paintings, such as Turner's "The Fighting *Temeraire*," Rosa Bonheur's "The Horse Fair," and Millet's "The Angelus." In my best penmanship I had written on white paper something about each painting and its creator, then carefully pasted the print and my composition first on gray construction paper, then on heavier dark blue, and finally bound the pages into a thick booklet with yarn, and printed my name, age, grade and school on the cover.

"Now, boys and girls, before we begin work, I want to tell you about another visitor, a friend of mine who came here yesterday. I showed him Mavis's art booklet, and he thought it was so good he left this note for her."

Miss Nikkinen held it out, clearly asking me to come up and get it. It seemed a very long moment before I could untangle my legs from the desk and walk to the front of the room with everyone looking at me. I hoped my petticoat wasn't showing.

"Open it, Mavis," urged Teacher.

I fumbled with the envelope and gasped at the sight of a two-dollar bill fluttering to the floor. While I read the brief note of congratulations, she spoke again. "Now, children, what do you think Mavis should do?"

"Buy us all candy," said Reino, breaking the ice. More suggestions came from around the room. "Buy a new sweater." "Go to twenty movies." "Save it for Christmas presents."

"I'm sure she will have no trouble deciding how to spend it—or save it," Teacher finally said. The slight frown line that showed when she was annoyed appeared between her eyebrows. "But what is the *polite* thing to do?"

I was silent with the rest.

"Remember, we have practiced writing different kinds of letters. What kind does this one call for?"

No one seemed to know, and I felt too dumbstruck to think.

"Oh, boys and girls, remember, a gift always calls for a thank you note. Will you write him one, Mavis?"

I felt my face turn hot. Conscious of having failed Teacher in an important way, I nodded and blinked back tears.

The eventful school day ended routinely. Teacher asked two boys to clean the blackboards and two others to go outside and bang the erasers together, two at a time, to release clouds of chalk dust. Two others filled the ink wells. Two girls emptied wastebaskets and the pencil sharpener. Teacher reminded us all to straighten out our desks and remember our homework before she pronounced "School dismissed," and we dashed for the cloakroom and the school busses.

Reino sat beside me. I felt his hand seek mine. I found a stick of Wrigley's Spearmint Gum in it. I glanced around to make sure no one had noticed. A boy friend guaranteed more teasing than anything else. I unwrapped the stick, slipped it into my mouth, and delighted in the first sweet minty spurt as the gum softened. The others chattered about The Giant Who Brings Lollipops to Good Little Citizens, but my silence seemed to discourage any mention of my own good fortune.

Suddenly I felt the bus tip over on its side and settle slowly and softly into a snowbank. I was sitting half on the floor, half sprawled against the bench, entangled with other kids. Elsie Miettunen was screaming because she had landed against the stove. The big boys lifted out the younger children, then helped Mr. Hujanen untangle the horses and harness. Slowly they righted the unwieldy bus and shoveled away the snow around it.

Some of the girls cried and exclaimed about how scared they had been. But I felt numb. I hadn't yet taken in the experience, so lost had I been in thinking about Mr. Barnes and the note. I felt in the palm of my hand, under the wet mitten, to make sure the money was still there.

"Weren't you scared?" Mamie asked.

"Not really." I wondered at my own strangeness. "If I'd known it was going to happen, I'd of been afraid beforehand. I always worry about what might happen. Mother calls me her Worry Wart. I imagine all kinds of things, and maybe have nightmares afterwards if something scary really happens. But she says I seem to be in another world when something's really happening."

We got back into the bus, and only the scorched wool of Elsie's coat reminded me that we had been in any danger.

I usually hated coming home on winter washdays, but today I was so eager to tell Mother all about the day that I hardly noticed Aino heaping the lines in the porch with frozen clothes from the outdoor lines, nor the heavy dampness of porch and kitchen, the sharp smell of Fels-Naphtha soap, the wet clothes draped in every available space. I threw my snowy wraps in the general direction of the woodbox, tore off my arctics, and was about to burst into the bedroom when Aino's cold hands gripped my shoulders. She said, "Hey! Your mother's asleep; now leave her alone. She said you kids gotta stay outta there until she calls you. Anyhow, you gotta carry wood. The box is almost empty. And then you gotta set the table and help me get supper. Gee whiz, if I'da known there was so much work in this house I never woulda taken this job."

Chores done and supper ready, waiting only for Father and Uncle Ray to come in, Mother called, "Come here, girls."

We cooed over the baby, who opened his eyes and looked at us very seriously. Then we interrupted each other telling about the excitement at school.

"Mother, when the Superintendent asked, Mabel knew what our national anthem is, and I think it's because you told us that when you were little you got up in front of the whole school and sang it and all the kids thought you were so brave."

"Mother, you never *saw* such a big man. And, Mother, guess what Mavis got?"

"She got a stupid look on her face when the bus tipped over in a snowbank and she just sat there chewing gum with her mouth open." It was Ray at the door, still smelling of the barn, never able to resist teasing.

"Oh, go jump in the lake!" I yelled. "Vic is a *good* brother. He doesn't make fun of me all the time like you do!" My big moment spoiled, I stamped angrily out of the room and up the stairs, my heavy brown shoes pounding each tread, a thick lump of resentment forming in my throat. I flopped on the floor to cry into the rag rug. Through the register I heard Mother softly scolding Ray. "You know how easily she's hurt, and she was feeling so happy."

"Well, she sure was, and she'd be better off and people would like her better if she wasn't so doggone proud of being so smart and being teacher's pet. She can't take any criticism; she always expects lots of praise."

I cried harder. Maybe what he said was true. And Ray was so handsome and athletic and witty that he was the most popular boy in school. Criticism from him was very hard to take.

"Yes, I suppose she *is* too sensitive," agreed Mother. "But she's like Victor. She takes school very seriously, and if everyone else studied as hard as she does, maybe she'd have more competition. Besides, you're her big brother. Don't you think you should try to make her happy instead of teasing her so much? Except for that, she thinks you're *wonderful*."

How I loved Mother at that moment. She understood me. Besides, she used big words that most of the other kids' mothers didn't know. She was "very Americanized," as she often proudly remarked, because she had been born in Minnesota, and her own mother had been a little girl when she came from Finland. Many of the other mothers in Vermilion had come as adults and knew very little English. Some still dressed peasant fashion in long dark dresses with white head scarves tied under their chins.

Mother had even let Uncle Arvid bob her hair when we visited his barber shop in Minneapolis. He backed her up when Father snorted at such foolishness. She retorted that she scarcely had time to keep a mop of heavy long hair clean, much less tidy, with all her work around the house and barn and garden. Father had kept sneaking glances at her all that evening. I could tell he liked how she looked after all.

When the bedroom was quiet again, I tiptoed in, sat on the side of the bed away from the baby, cuddled close to Mother, and whispered the story of the two dollars and the lesson in politeness.

"What a day you had, with Mr. Barnes and the lollipops, your note and the two dollars, and the bus tipping over! Thank goodness it didn't catch fire from that old stove. And here I've just been a lazy bum, lying in bed with the baby. But that's the only time I get a vacation—when I have a new baby."

"And Mother, what Ray said. It's not true. I don't always expect praise. It sometimes makes me feel shy and embarrassed. And I *hate* to be called teacher's pet."

"Just don't care if they do. I was teacher's pet too, I guess. But if that means the teacher thinks you're smart and work hard, then the other kids are just being jealous. Say to yourself, 'Sticks and stones may break my bones, But names will never hurt me.' Now here's a kiss to show you how much I love you and how proud I am of you."

I dried my tears on the warm softness of Mother's nightgown and got up to join the family at supper. And when Ray was looking the other way, I stuck out my tongue at him.

Floods and Flowers

Just when we were saying winter would never end, spring came with a rush of melting snow. The brook flooded to a small lake. Roads were impassable by car. The schools declared "mud vacation."

Mabel helped Father and the boys—except Vic, whose school was unaffected by country roads—pick rocks turned up by winter frost and load them onto the sledge, clearing the fields for plow and disk and harrow.

I was in bed with one of my sore throats and earaches. Mother had heated a bag of salt in the oven to place over my ear, wrapped my throat with a piece of flannel and a wool sock, rubbed my chest with Vicks Vapo-Rub and tucked a large square of wool over it, under my nightgown. She had dosed me with a tablespoonful of cream to which she added two or three drops of turpentine, and when I said "Ish!" she promised to give me Pinex syrup instead if I didn't stop coughing.

Though I protested that nothing tasted good, I was happy when she brought me bowlfuls of hot milk toast flavored with onions and butter, and a sweet soup made of dried apricots, prunes, apples and raisins, thickened with tapioca and laced with sweet cream.

I passed the hours writing about her pioneer days on the homestead land five miles away, in the one-room log cabin that was now the bedroom. As a nineteen-year-old mother, she stayed there with her first baby for fourteen months. Father was seldom home; he worked on the county road in summer and in the Tower sawmill in winter. He was there when Ray was born, and had to fetch help, and when he milked the cow, she stuck her foot in the pail. Before Bobby was born, Mother had told us these stories when we were sick in bed. She often got a faraway look in her eyes when she thought of those "pioneer days."

And I read whatever was at hand. I still loved the Teeny Weenies, who lived in a shoe at the bottom of a garden, and admired the exquisite courtesy of the men, peg-legged Captain, young Sailor, and all, toward the Lady of Fashion. I suffered with the passengers on the *Titanic* until Mother took the book away for fear it would give me one of my nightmares.

Dozing one afternoon, I was wakened by Mabel's fierce sobbing and shouting. "I know he did it! Mr. Miettunen shot Miksi! He's a mean man!"

I wrapped the quilt around myself and went downstairs. Mabel's pink-and-white skin was blotched with red and streaked with tears. Coming from the field, she had found the dog's body near the road, and her fury took in everyone around, but was directed mostly at the neighbor on the hill. Mother cuddled her in the rocking chair and tried to comfort her.

"Well, you know, honey, he said Miksi got after his chickens and he warned us about that. There was just no way we could keep him away from them without chaining him up, and you wanted him to go everywhere with you. We'll find you another dog. And I heard some new kittens up in the hayloft this morning."

As Mabel went on sobbing, Mother harked back to her own childhood, as she often did when a child was sad or angry. "On the last day of first grade we had a program. Mama was there. I held a doll and recited a poem:

> Suppose, my little lady,
> Your doll should break her head,
> Could you make it whole by crying
> Till your eyes and nose were red?
> And wouldn't it be better,

And by far the very best plan,
Whatever comes and doesn't come,
To do the best you can?"

The verse comforted Mabel. I know it was a comfort to Mother all her long life. Now Mabel said, snuffling, "We'll call the new dog Miksi too. Because it's such fun to have a dog named 'Why?' in Finn. When people ask why we named him Miksi, we can say *'Siksi'*—because!"

❊❊❊❊❊❊❊❊❊❊❊❊

Bobby was baptized on Easter Sunday, to take advantage of the Rev. Mr. Heino's coming to preach an Easter sermon at the little Evangelical Lutheran church by the river. The sun was bright though trees were still bare. The ground had dried and the brook was almost down to normal.

By noon the house sparkled, and the kitchen table was set with our best white cloth, glossy with starch. The four plump roosters the boys had killed and plucked were roasting in the oven.

The young minister greeted Father and Mother and Grandpa in Finnish, the younger generation in English. He placed a lectern by the bedroom window to the west, where Norway pines glistened through the sheer white curtain.

Aunt Hilma held the baby in his long white dress while the minister prayed. Then he took the baby and touched his head with water, blessing him in the name of the Father, the Son and the Holy Ghost. His soft blond hair, his gentle, placid young face, his stiff white collar with two tabs in front over the high buttoned vest of his black suit—all these made him seem special and holy. When he raised his blue eyes heavenward, his hand resting on the baby's head, and asked for the blessing of God on the new Christian, in the long vowels and rolling r's of the Finnish language, I hugged my arms around my shoulders to calm my goose pimples.

The minister himself relaxed the solemn mood. He handed the now howling baby to Aunt Hilma and said, "Well, now George Robert Hiltunen is a new little Lutheran and it sounds as if he's just as hungry as I am. Those sure are good smells coming from the kitchen!"

Grandpa and all the aunts and uncles sat down with the

minister and Mother and Father. Victor had insisted that today Mother was nobody's servant, and the young cousins would help us wait on table.

Before they began to eat, the grownups all bowed their heads and waited for the Rev. Heino to ask a blessing on the food. Why didn't we do this every day, I wondered. Perhaps we so seldom all sat down together, ready to eat at the same time, that only on special occasions like this was there time for it. Mother was often milking when Father and the younger children ate; the bigger boys might still be out trapping or fishing or playing ball, and not come home till after dark . . .

"Hey, Mavis! Stop dreaming. We need more mashed potatoes and gravy, and some cranberry relish to go with this wonderful chicken." Uncle Felix's grin and wink told me he understood. I guess Mother's not the only one who gets that faraway look, I thought. Maybe I'm like her. But I don't think I'd be brave enough to live alone in the woods with a small baby. I hope I'll be a good cook, though. My uncle's smile and hug inspired me to check all the serving dishes and replenish the food.

❊❊❊❊❊❊❊❊❊❊❊

Mother's Day was another sunny spring day, flooded with special Sunday brightness. It also happened to be Mother's birthday.

Right after breakfast each of us kids brought out a bouquet of trailing arbutus. In our free time Saturday we had climbed down into the ravines and up the pine-clad hills behind the house. There we hunted tiny pink blossoms flush on the ground among their small stiff leaves. We often found a patch of arbutus near the edge of a stubbornly frozen patch of spongy gray snow. Every year Mother expressed great delight over each child's offering and took deep ecstatic breaths of the sweet fragrance as she arranged the clusters in vases.

Mother turned back to her baking. She was making Father's and my favorite pastry: light, flaky rolls filled with apple, raisins, sugar, cinnamon, and butter. Father clasped her around the waist from behind and rubbed his unshaven cheek against hers. "I like this smell better than arbutus," he said.

Then he sang a Finnish birthday song that was reminiscent of their wedding day.

"You grew, charming maiden, in your father's cabin,
Like a lovely sweet flower in the grass."

Mother blushed and laughed, and gave him a little push
with her floury hands. "Go and shave. You should have done it
in the sauna last night."

In the afternoon we all dressed up for the Mother's Day
program at school—all except Victor, who had a free day but
rebelled against "sitting through all that boring stuff, the same
old junk year after year."

"I suppose you'd rather play cards at Matt's camp," said
Mother, resigned.

"You darn right I would," he said loudly as he banged out
the door.

A short, serious, and extremely proper missionary couple
led the religious observance. I liked the Rev. Mr. Stanway. Behind his rimless glasses his blue eyes shone with fervor, and his
jug ears turned red with the warmth of his preaching, though
he never ranted and raved like some Finnish preachers. I was
sure he meant every word. Sometimes missionaries came to
the house—often very close to mealtime—and their particularly
sanctimonious way of saying, "Shall we bow our heads?" sent
me sneaking up to my hideaway, "The Little Floor."

Sweet, prim Mrs. Stanway, her graying hair softly waved
and parted in the middle and drawn into a knot at the back,
pumped the portable organ for the hymns. Though the Stanways
spoke only English, almost all the parents came, because the
teachers had drilled all the children in songs and recitations.

I wondered why some of the mothers covered their mouths
with their handkerchiefs and looked mirthfully at one another
during some pieces that seemed beautifully sentimental to me.
One was a song we sang every year:

M is for the million things she gave me;
O means only that she's growing old;
T is for the tears she shed to save me;
H is for her heart of purest gold;
E is for her eyes with lovelight shining;
R means right, and right she'll always be;
Put them all together, they spell MOTHER,
The sweetest word in all the world to me.

I felt tearful when Charlie Hujanen from eighth grade recited "Somebody's Mother," about a woman who was old and tattered and gray, and bent with the chill of the winter's day; when a boy helped her cross the street, a prosperous-looking gentleman asked him if she were his mother, and "She's Somebody's Mother, sir," he said. Then I too had to stiffle a giggle when Aili whispered, "Yeah, his mother is *somebody's* mother, all right—his and Kerttu's and Leslie's" . . . and so on through thirteen more names.

After his closing prayer, Rev. Stanway smiled at the audience, rubbed his hands together, and said, "Now isn't it time for some of that wonderful Finnish coffee bread?" I thought ministers must be especially adept at switching from serious thoughts about God to lighter thoughts of food.

※-꒷꒦꒷꒦-꒷꒦꒷-꒷꒦꒷-꒷꒦꒷※

The last weeks of school brought a foretaste of freedom. During lunch hour Aili and I caught tadpoles in the swollen ditches, or took pieces of reed from the stockroom where the basket-weaving supplies were kept, and smoked them on mossy rocks under the budding birch trees behind the school. They tasted awful; the fun was all in feeling wicked. Sometimes there was just enough time to run to the "Kwap" or Salmela's store for candy before afternoon classes.

The sounds of the eighth graders' preparation for their graduation ceremony lightened the chores of cleaning out desks and returning books for Teacher to examine for damage. As I plied my eraser I was sorry I had so thoughtlessly doodled profiles and lips and hearts on the margins of the older books.

Finally came the word "Dismissed!" with a broad smile and a long sigh of relief from Teacher. We erupted from the school yelling, "No more pencils, no more books, no more Teacher's cross-eyed looks!"

Three rural schools joined forces for the graduation ceremonies that night at Pike Hall. Mabel and I agreed that Ray was the handsomest boy of all. His dark blond hair, parted in the middle, was carefully combed into a gleaming wave at each side. His new tan tweed suit, which would also have to do for confirmation next year, was a bit too big, but his white shirt glistened with starch and his bow tie was debonair. As always he shone with perfect grooming, all scrubbed, manicured, and polished.

And his tenor voice! It carried the tunes so beautifully when they sang the familiar songs of graduation:

Welcome, sweet springtime, we greet thee in so-ong,
Murmurs of gladness fall on the ea-ear;
Voices long hushed now their glad notes
prolo-ong,
Echoing far and near.

But I thought that "Aloha Oe," with its sentimental, mournful strains, its sadness at parting, was even more beautiful:

Proudly sweeps the rain cloud o'er the cliff,
Borne swiftly by the western gale,
While the song of lovers' parting grief
Sadly echoes amid the flow'ring vale.

Aili and I giggled because we knew Miss Kochevar had told the eighth graders to sing "classmates" instead of "lovers," and they had schemed to fool her. The teachers tried to look cross, but I caught a wink between two of them.

Farewell to thee, farewell to thee,
The winds will carry back my sad refra-ain,
One fond embrace, before we say goodbye,
Until we me-he-heet again.

When I graduated, I mused, I would be sure to give the valedictory speech, and would wear a pink silk dress. But I wouldn't be one bit nervous, as the girl had been tonight, her voice high and quivery. And neither would I, despite the sentimental songs, be very sorry to part from my schoolmates. Most of us would see each other again in high school. Besides, I would meet lots of new kids, and many of them wouldn't be Finns. That would make me feel more Americanized.

And I pictured myself, some day, as a teacher organizing just such a graduation ceremony. In his address, Mr. Barnes had again assured us that in America you could be anything you wanted to be if you worked hard.

Peeper frogs chorused from the misty meadow by the brook as we got out of the car at home. The moon was nearly full. Life was beautiful. Tomorrow, I thought, I would pick some swamp laurel for the table and try once more to make a bouquet of buttercups—Teacher called them marsh marigolds—last for more than an hour without drooping. I knew where a glowing golden carpet of them stretched as far as I could see under the trees of the swamp, the way the free days of summer stretched ahead.

Father and Mother in their everyday clothes.

Milk, Butter and Eggs

June, as I remember it, was idyllic. Potatoes were already planted, but blueberries were not yet ripe nor hay ready for scythe and mower. Everything was still fresh and new, and Mabel and I felt like the young calves frisking in the barnyard. When Mother didn't need us for chores, we were free to roam. Our bare feet were tickled by pine needles in the woods on the hillside and by new grass in the fields, cooled by the squishy mud of the golden-weedy brook, hardened by the gravel of the roads, dusty from the soft powdery paths that cut through the fields, and soon too big for our clumpy brown school shoes. Our hair turned platinum blonde in the sun, our skin brown where our bib overalls left it bare.

The first clear day after school was out—usually around Decoration Day—everyone had pitched in to plant potatoes. No one had to be reminded that we ate potatoes at least once a day all year round. Hour after hour we set the carefully cut pieces with an eye or potential plant right side up in the furrow Father and Vic had prepared with the hiller plow. By evening the smoke rising from the sauna chimney beckoned us to wash off the dust and the potato smell and bake out the aches from bending over all day long. We wolfed down Mother's hearty *mojakka* stew and rhubarb pie, and before long, snores, gentle or sonorous, chorused a fugue in the moonlit house.

For two days a week the everlasting washing also had priority over play, but out in the fresh air by the sauna it was pure pleasure compared to a winter washday. The boys started a fire in the small cast-iron stove of the sauna dressing room, set the big copper boiler on top, and filled it with water they carried from pump to sauna, pail after pail. Then they filled the two big galvanized iron tubs on the stand that stood in the grass near the sauna door. It looked like two huge wooden chairs back to back, with the upright wringer in between.

Mother shaved slices from a bar of Fels-Naphtha Soap, so strong it stung my nose, into the boiler. She stirred the clothes in the boiling water with a thick wooden pole like a baseball bat. She lifted the steaming clothes into a tub and showed us how to scrub them on the metal washboard with another bar of golden-yellow soap. We scrubbed till our arms grew tired and Mother took pity on us.

I turned the wringer handle while Mabel fed the soapy clothes between the thick rubber rollers into the other tub for the first rinse.

I tossed my head in annoyance as Leo went by, scoffing from his superior masculine height (he was now a chunky twelve-year-old) "Yeah, girls, that's the way to build muscles!"

"Oh, shut up, you ball-headed. . ."

Vic and Ray were already aware of girls, and no longer clipped their hair to the scalp as soon as school was out, but Leo was still young enough to prefer coolness and freedom.

Through the wringer once more, into the second rinse water, a rich blue from a generous dollop of French's Blueing to heighten their whiteness, and again through the wringer before we could shake out the clothes and hang them on the lines stretched from the sauna wall to a T-post.

We laughed as the wind flapped wet diapers into our faces. The sky was so blue, the breeze so alive, and the sun so warm that work became play, and I didn't even mind Father's joking that if I stretched enough to pin the clothes on the line I'd grow faster.

While each line dried, Mother let us off to explore the woods behind the house, wade in the brook, or push each other in the swing under a tall pine tree.

Or to fetch the mail. If it was very close to mail time, Mother handed us a small bundle of penny postcards and letters with two-cent stamps stuck in the corner, and told us to run like sixty. Our new Miksi at our heels, we clambered over the near gate, ran over the little hill to the far gate, turned left onto the township road along the edge of Miettunens' farm, and climbed the steep Big Hill. Atop it, we could see the row of three mailboxes on the county road. If the mailman's car was there, we waved our letters and ran to give them to him. If not, we skipped down the sharp dip before the last hill and stopped to sniff the wild roses and notice where columbine grew to pick for Mother on the way home, and to nibble a few of their round points full of nectar. If the mailman still hadn't come, and we wanted to explore the woods, we left the letters in the mailbox and turned up the red metal flag so that the mailman would know there were letters inside.

Father was usually waiting impatiently in the rocking chair for the *Päivälehti* and *Duluth Herald* and *Co-op Builder*, which he and Vic read over mid-morning coffee. Bathed and changed into the clothes we had dried, Bobby was playing in the pen Vic had concocted in the shade of the house. He seldom needed attention. We knew we had to take down the rest of the sweet fresh diapers and fold them into the bushel basket before we could play. Perhaps we also had to fetch "about five sifters of whole wheat flour and three of white" from the cool dark *puoji*. Mabel stood on a stool and reached down into the bins where hundred-pound sacks of flour had been emptied, and counted the sifterfuls into the huge tin bread pan I held.

Then we escaped to the light shade of the budding, blossoming woods on the hill behind the house. We found fragile velvety mauve hepaticas and delicate pink and white anemones, mayflowers, ordinary purple violets and the rarer fragrant white ones nearly hidden under last year's leaves. Bird songs lured us to hunt for nests of tiny eggs or hungry beaks.

Day by day we watched the small white blossoms of wild strawberries in the low thin grass on the hillside shed their petals and give way to hard greenish-white balls that ripened a bright red. For a few days there were only enough to pick straight into our mouths. Then we took coffee cups to fill and ate them with cream and sugar. We shared them with Mother and Father; the boys would find their own. For hours our hands were pink and perfumed, no matter how often we washed them.

Mother sometimes straightened up from thinning a bed of lettuce or carrots, rubbed her back, looked up at the scudding white clouds in the bright blue sky, and declaimed:

What is so rare as a day in June?
Then, if ever, come perfect days.

Or sang, in her sweet uncertain voice,

Sing, bird, up in the apple tree,
Hum, bee, over the rose,
Laugh, brook, ripple in melody,
Sweet little buds, unclose.
Wave, grass, up in the valley wide,
Leap high, grasshopper gay,
Dear flowers, never one chalice hide,
Summer will never stay.

To me, however, summer seemed to stretch on and on into the future, each day more full of delight and wonder than the last. We knew every cherry tree and sugar-plum bush in the woods, every promising blueberry patch in pastures and cut-over land, every brambly tangle of blossoming raspberry vine. Dandelions were bright golden treasures to weave into crowns or carry in sap-stained hands to Mother, who put them in glasses of water where their glory soon faded. When their heads turned downy white in the grass, we would pick one and ask, "Tell me, pretty maiden, does my mother want me home?" Then we had to give one hard puff; it wasn't fair to blow gently. If all the seeds blew away, it was time to go home. If not, we lay a while longer in the grass, imagined shapes of monsters and castles and angels in the clouds, or watched ants, bees, and butterflies go about their business.

I liked to look under toadstools for elves and imagine I found fairy rings. But Mabel liked to climb to the top of the tallest Norway pine on the hill and shout down to me as I stood timidly below, "I can see Tower and Ely and Virginia and Duluth."

"Aw, you liar, liar, pants on fire, nose as long as a telephone wire! All you can see is Miettunens' house and the potato field and the haylofts in the meadow."

The long summer twilights invited visiting and games and romping and gossip. After milking time a car or two loaded with whole families would turn down our road. While the ladies helped Mother fix coffee, the men played horseshoes or sat on the grass until the mosquitoes drove them indoors. The children played shrieking games of hide-and-seek and tag. We threw a softball over the house, yelling "Anti-Anti-I-Over!" to the team on the other side. The boys played catch and softball far enough from the house to avoid warnings about windows.

The girls held hands in a circle. Then, leaning farther and farther away from each other, we turned in dizzying circles, hair flying, feet close together, until our hands pulled apart and we fell down in the grass, panting and laughing, flushed, and conscious of our young bodies only as instruments we used and enjoyed. We rolled over and over down the slope, sniffed the camomile flowers and clover, laughed and squealed. We screamed as it grew dark and bats swooped.

One afternoon when Mother was milking, Mabel and I sat on the front steps with Bobby and pouted about the boys' freedom to go fishing on the river. Mosquitoes hummed around our bare legs furiously. When Mother called "Gur-ruls!" Mabel took the baby in and I ran down to the barn. I pushed aside the gunnysack curtain that was supposed to keep horseflies away from the

Our barnyard: privy, barn, gate to Krapus' lane, stable with cows and our sturdy horses in the foreground.

cows. Mother was sitting on a three-legged stool, her kerchiefed head bent against Kirjonen's dark brown flank, and I heard alternating streams of milk striking the sides of the pail with a rhythmic hiss and plink. Trying not to breathe too deeply of the urine-manure-hay scented air, I crossed the straw-strewn concrete floor and stood beside Mother until she looked up.

I couldn't bring myself to complain, but she noticed that I was in a bad mood, and remembered that we had pouted when she had let the boys go to the river. But she said only, "Oh, I'm glad you came. Bring my other shoes and a clean dress and apron in case visitors come before I'm through milking."

She often asked us to do this, because she hurried to milk the cows, "dressed any old way" as she said, in an old housedress and runover men's shoes with traces of manure and straw clinging to them, and a scarf tied behind her ears. As she milked, one possible visitor after another occurred to her—and if her upper lip itched, she was sure someone would come. She also believed that if a visitor came on Monday—even the Watkins man, with his vanilla and spices—we would have company every day that week.

"Now run along, and get those things, and cheer up. You'll grow up fast enough. How about a squirt of *lämmiä*?" she said.

I opened my mouth wide for our old game, and she expertly shot a stream of Kirjonen's warm milk into it. She smiled, pushed out her false upper teeth, sucked them back in, and bent her head to the cow's round brown side once more. As I stooped to slip between the poles of the barnyard gate and trudged up the short slope to the house, I wished we had never laughed at Mother's trick with her teeth. It was comical, but what if she forgot and did it when we had company? She really looked nice when she combed her hair and was happy. And she always had a fresh dress and apron ready. And I felt less put upon and more helpful, because I realized how hard Mother worked and how much she needed our help—though there still were times when I forgot.

Next day Andrew Kahtava, who was a clever carpenter, began to put wood siding on the house, with Victor as his helper. I was glad we wouldn't live in an old-fashioned log cabin anymore, but I would miss seeing the cabin Mother had lived in on the homestead land, which was now the bedroom. Most of us had been born in that cabin, and it wouldn't feel the same. I went around to the cool shade back of the house and leaned my head

Top: Our house in the spring of 1917, with Mother, Father, Leo, Victor and Ray. Bottom: The same log house but with wood siding and a porch. This is how it looked for many years.

against a silvery gray log, picked at a sliver of wood, and wondered how I could be both happy and sad at the same time.

Vic came around the corner with a sawhorse. He usually knew what I was thinking. He glanced at me, smiled, and then looked serious.

"It's really a shame to cover up this old work. These pioneer cabins are made the old Finnish way. See how the logs are squared off with broad axes and fitted so tightly you need hardly

The sauna, showing the dove-tailed corners and the old copper washboiler on the side wall.

any mortar? See this dovetailing at the corners? But Maw wants the house to look modern, like those in town, and we have to paint it white after we get this siding on. Hey, I hear her calling you."

Churning time. Mother licked the finger she had dipped into the cream can to see that it was just right—not too sweet and not yet turning sour. "It's going to be very hot today so I want to make the butter early. You girls take turns churning."

She set the big red barrel churn on its stand, locked it into place, poured in the cream, and made sure she snapped the lid tightly shut. I found a fat red book to read during the boring chore and sat down to turn the wooden handle round and round. The cream sloshed and splashed. The book was one Vic had borrowed from the Virginia Public Library—Zane Grey's *The Vanishing American*. Soon I was so engrossed in it that I turned the handle more and more slowly, stopped to turn a page and forgot to churn for a while, until Mother noticed and took away the book.

When my arm was tired, Mabel took her turn. The day was warm, and it wasn't long before the liquid splashing was punctuated by the thud of lumps, and small yellow balls of butter stuck to the little glass window in the lid. "Mother, now it's kerplunking and not just sloshing around," said Mabel.

Now her arms were tired, and I took over. It was a little harder to turn the handle now, but I persisted until Mother decided the lumps were large enough to work.

Several times she dipped out as much butter as she could with a long-handled strainer and plopped it into the huge shallow wooden bowl that smelled of countless weeks of butter making. Then she tipped the churn to drain the buttermilk and capture any remaining butter. She rewarded us with glasses of buttermilk and slabs of bread and jam.

We watched her rinse the butter until the water ran clear, and work it with her flat wooden paddle between rinses. When it was free of water, we liked to watch her shape it into deep rippled folds. She turned and turned the bowl and tilted out every last drop of water. As she worked the butter, she worked and pursed her lips in rhythm too, and when she heard us giggling, she turned and caught us mocking her, and pushed out her teeth at us.

Last of all, she carefully poured salt into the palm of her hand, sprinkled it on the butter, worked it in, and tasted it several times until she was satisfied that it was just salty enough. We were proud of Mother's expert way with butter. In some houses, the butter tasted strong and sour, but hers was always mild and sweet.

Saturday was cream day. We were very busy until Mother got off to town. We had to scrub pint and quart bottles with a brush in soapy water, scald them, fill them carefully with rich yellow cream, wipe off the drips, and firmly stick a cardboard cap in each opening. We were too small to be trusted with the five-pound stone crocks for butter, or even the smaller ones, but we liked watching Mother deftly work it into every bit of space before she tied a double layer of wax paper on top.

If the hens had laid enough, we washed eggs and carefully put them into cartons. If there was fresh buttermilk left over, we bottled that too, for there was no dairy in Tower and every drop was welcome.

❈❈❈❈❈❈❈❈❈❈❈

One Saturday Aunt Hilma was at the farm and offered to look after Bobby so that Mabel and I could go to town. We hurried to change into our new sandals and sundresses, because Father, impatient as always, was already honking the horn.

We sat in back, holding the eggs carefully, and watched for the moment when we crossed a little bridge in the long meadow between Hendricksons' and Wahlstens', with its high bump that gave us a roller-coaster thrill as the car swooped and settled and our stomachs seemed to flip over. Then we were in the pine forest, and chorused, "Pretty soon downtown!" Mother turned to look at us, and laughed. "Did you know its founder's name was Charlemagne Tower?" Before there was time for her to explain why she found it so amusing, we were there.

The sign at the edge of town boasted that the Incorporated City of Tower, founded in 1884, had 700 inhabitants. For Mabel and me it was civilization. Its eight-block-long Main Street looked almost exactly like the town in a cowboy movie we had seen. False-front business buildings lined both sides: the Rex Theater, the post office, grocery and hardware stores, the city hall, the

The Rex Movie Theater in Tower, Minnesota.

The main street of Tower, Minnesota.

office of the *Tower Weekly News,* a couple of gas station-ga-
rages, and the small hotel-restaurant where Vic had worked.
A block off Main Street were the Immanuel Lutheran Church
and the Catholic Church, both of which looked huge compared
to our little white church by the river. And the red brick schools
looked enormous. The elementary school was at least four times
the size of School 40, and the Tower-Soudan High School had to
be large enough to serve not only Tower, but also Soudan, only
a mile away, near the deepest underground mine in the world,
where Uncles Ray and Felix worked.

At one end of Main Street stood a small gray obelisk with
a plaque honoring President William McKinley. When I was
handing Vic nails the day before, he had told me, "You may not
think so much of Tower now that you've been to Minneapolis,
but it was five times as big as it is now when the iron mines were
first operating, and the first shipment of iron ore went from
there to Two Harbors in 1884. Besides, it was the first town in
the whole country to put up a monument to President McKinley
after he was assassinated."

Then, of course, he had to explain assassinations, and
Abraham Lincoln, and plead coffee time to escape my intermi-
nable questions.

Tower stands at the east end of huge pine-fringed and island-dotted Lake Vermilion. This June day a few out-of-state licenses signaled that the tourist season had begun. Lake cottage owners had arrived for the summer, and fishermen were hauling boats to their favorite camps. In town, a few farmers were shopping for things they couldn't find at the local Co-op, and housewives were planning their Sunday dinners.

For a while Father took Mother around to various customers, and at one house, he carried out a small table she had paid for with cream. When the racks of bottles were light enough for Mother and Mabel and me to carry, he told us to meet him at the IGA grocery store in an hour and went off on his own errands.

I liked to visit the city ladies with their electric lights and indoor bathrooms, their uncluttered glassed-in porches that were inviting places to relax and visit rather than to store the overflow of a farmhouse—and especially their fine English, which sounded almost affected to my ears, but which I did my best to imitate when I was alone. But I felt bashful around them.

Mother, however, seemed perfectly happy and at home with them. She knew just what to say and how to say it, I thought, with the same tone and inflection, and not a trace of Finnish brogue. She considered all her customers her friends. During her erratic periods of schooling, many had been her classmates, and they seemed glad to see her and buy her wares. Mrs. Pryor was airing and sunning winter clothes and getting summer ones ready.

"I put aside a few that Billy and Betty have outgrown," she said. "I wonder if any of your children might be able to use them?"

I was proud of the dignified way Mother answered, smiling, "Oh, thank you, Amanda. I'm sure they can."

But I did wonder why she had only two children, and so many other families in Tower were much smaller than ours. Before I could ask about it, a woman approached on Main Street, and Mother greeted her, "Why, hello, Elsie."

The woman apparently found the dusty jumble of goods in the hardware store window so fascinating that she didn't hear her. For a moment Mother's face looked like a storm cloud. Then she strode briskly on.

I asked, "Is that lady deaf, Mother?"

"No, she's *not* deaf! She's someone I knew when we were girls and she doesn't like to admit she's Finnish. And she's so *mad* at me for marrying a greenhorn!"

"What's a greenhorn?"

She was still angry. "Oh, somebody *dumb*, I guess."

"But Father's not one bit dumb. He's smart."

"Well, I mean she looked down on him because he was so fresh from the Old Country and his English was so poor. Hmph! She's just *too proud!*"

Although bright red spots still burned on Mother's cheeks, she held her head high as she greeted Mrs. Kitto, her next customer. During sixth grade, Mother had lived with her and helped with the baby and the housework to earn her room and board, and they were close friends.

Her bottle racks empty, Mother headed for her old friend Celia Soper's, where she knew a good coffee awaited her. "Here's a nickel for each of my good helpers. Be back in fifteen minutes."

We ran to Martilla's Drug Store and used up five of those minutes agonizing over which flavor of ice cream we should buy—vanilla, chocolate, or strawberry. Each tongueful, so luscious! How precious each drip that had to be licked up quickly from the side of the cone on this hot day! Was there ever ice cream as good as old Konst Marttila's?

At the grocery store Father stuck his hands deep in his pockets and looked away while Mother shopped for things he didn't approve of—delicacies he thought foolish, like canned pineapple and coconut, walnuts and chocolate, and the gooey marshmallow-topped cookies iced with pink or white or chocolate and sprinkled with chopped coconut that we kids considered a great treat. I was glad that here he dared not berate her for her extravagance, as he sometimes did at the Co-op. She asked him to pay only for the cans of Campbell's Pork and Beans and the wienies for supper. She paid for the rest.

Mother managed to provide us with all kinds of things we would never have had without her business—not only goodies to eat, but also secondhand furniture like the table, an organ she got for $10, and eventually a radio. And later, an occasional life-saving $5 bill found its way into letters to me at college. Best of all, I am sure, it gave her a sense of pride in her own accomplishments, and a legitimate excuse to go to town and see her old friends.

Every June, Bible School interrupted our long free days. We had to walk to School 40 every morning for a week, Finnish catechisms in hand. There the Rev. Mr. Aho drilled us in such basics as the Apostles' Creed, The Lord's Prayer, and the Ten Commandments. He was so serious about our learning to write and speak Finnish correctly that he sometimes shook his head in despair, and hardly ever spoke English except to explain a difficult passage.

When he heard us speaking Finglish, he shook his finger at us and exclaimed, "Beti! Haussi! Puuka! Say bed, house, book. Or say *sänky, talo, kirja*. Speak either English or Finnish, but don't mix them up."

Not all the school kids were there. Some went to the Apostolic Lutheran Church, whose pastors were usually far from mild-mannered like ours, but shouted and threatened with hellfire and brimstone anyone who danced or played cards or went to the movies. Some kids, like Aili, didn't go to church or Bible school at all. Aili showed me one day a composition she had written for classes at Vermilion Hall; it was all about the evolution of the earth, not at all like a Bible lesson. Mother sometimes shook her head and tightened her lips about that, but it didn't bother me, perhaps because I had so often heard Father say that Finns were alike in many ways but had a right to be different in many others. He attended church only on ceremonial occasions, and smilingly tolerated Mother as *uskovainen*—a believer.

But Vic's attitude did disturb me a little. One day Eino, his friend, walked part way with us to Bible School. I heard him teasing Vic. "You still going to Bible School like a little kid?"

Vic answered, "Oh, I know it's a lot of bullshit, but I'll never hear the end of it if I don't get confirmed next year. Father thinks everyone's just a kid until he's been through *rippikoulu*. And you know how religious Mother is."

❄❄❄❄❄❄❄❄❄❄

On Saturday morning Mother observed that our hair was so long it was getting into our eyes, and gave each of us a dime to run over to Charlie Niemi's for a haircut, so we'd look nice for Sunday's closing program.

"Niemi Kalle" often came to sauna, and I liked to watch him clamber out of his 1922 Model T roadster, walk slowly around

it twice, and kick each tire as he made the circuit. Despite his
shyness, he never failed to come out with a modest proposal over
sauna coffee. Speaking very deliberately, but with a slight smile,
he looked into his cup and said, "*Pekka*, if you ever leave your
wife a widow, I'll marry her. She's so clean and such a good cook."

Mother winked at us and tried not to laugh, but I thought
she was a bit flattered just the same.

One evening in sauna she explained to us why there were
so many bachelors in the neighborhood. "Charlie was quite good
looking when he was younger, with that red hair, those blue eyes,
and that dimple in his chin," she said. "But many more young
men came from Finland than girls, and not all of them found
wives here, especially those who didn't know any English—and
you know how poor Charlie's English is. And he's so shy and
quiet—and a little slow."

Our carpenter, Andrew, drank a lot, and Elias Keranen,
though he was as clean as any housewife, was a loner who preferred to read and meditate, and never showed up at social affairs. And Matt—well, Matt tried marriage, but that's another
story.

Charlie's four-room house was clapboarded and painted,
and the inside was spacious and light, and we marveled that it
was so much nicer and cleaner than Matt's. It was a bit stuffy
because Charlie was mortally afraid of drafts. People said he
put on suit after suit of long underwear as the weather got colder,
and peeled them off one by one in the spring. He wore a copper
bracelet in the belief that it would alleviate rheumatic pain.

The smells of yellowing newspapers piled on the Finnish-
style benches around the walls, and of chewing tobacco and spit-
toons, were inoffensive compared to Matt's cabin. Besides, Charlie played the violin, a much more elegant instrument than the
accordion. The boys said they sometimes heard beautiful strains
of music at night, and crept up to listen as close as they dared.
If he heard them, he put his fiddle away at once.

Charlie hummed softly as he plied scissors and clippers,
walking around and around the chair until he was satisfied with
the Dutch bob he had created. We were impatient at his slow-
ness and his shaky hands, and after we surrendered our dimes
we ran home, shaking our heads—they felt so light!—and stopping to blow away the tickly hairs on each other's necks that
had escaped his towel and brush. We savored a few mouthfuls
of strawberries and noted where they grew most thickly.

The Bible School program was solemn and low key. We showed off what we had learned to our smiling parents, who were happy to hear us speaking correct Finnish. We tried to sing the slow chants or *virsis* printed in Gothic type in the small old hymnals while Elsie Dahl played the organ.

After the usual coffee in the church kitchen and visiting on the church lawn, we headed home. Father started another *virsi*, and since the tunes were all about the same, we chanted as best we could. The oft-repeated words mingled sadness and thankfulness. I concentrated on the vowels which stretched out especially long in these chants. "God" became "*Juuu-maaa-laaa*" and "in Heaven" was "*taaaii-vaaass-saaa.*"

When the sun shone down in wide golden rays from behind a gray-blue cloud, radiating like the halos in pictures of Old Man God sitting on His throne in the heavens, I thought God must be happy to hear us praising Him.

But the holy mood didn't last. While Mother was changing into barn clothes and we undressed Bobby, Vic also changed clothes and slipped out to Matt's camp, where a few boys would doubtless play cards and drink home brew. Getting what Mother called a "lap" of firewood to make supper, I heard her singing, "Oh Happy Day, that fixed my choice, On Thee, my Saviour and my God," while she milked the cows. Despite the words, her singing sounded melancholy, and I wondered if she ever felt lonely even with the whole family around, the way I sometimes did.

I picked a bouquet of pansies from her flower garden and put it on the supper table. I look deep into their pensive little faces and hoped Mother would say, as she often did, that they were smiling at her.

"Forchuly"

Independence Day was Father's favorite holiday, next to the Finnish Midsummer's Day. We adopted his Finglish pronunciation, and to us it was always "Forchuly."

He found the cluster of five little American flags he kept from year to year, and fastened it to the radiator cap of our Ford car. On the way to Tower, their fluttering signaled that here was a car full of Americans proclaiming their patriotism.

"I never saw so many people in Tower before," marveled Mabel.

"Last year it rained," Mother reminded her, "but today it's perfect Forchuly weather."

Everyone was there—whole families, bachelors, workmen, the young, the old, townsfolk, country people. Immigrants from Yugoslavia, Czechoslovakia, Italy, Sweden, Norway, Finland—most of them naturalized Americans like Father—and their children and grandchildren. A few families who had followed the westward call from New England and bore old British names. Indians from the Chippewa reservation, in full tribal regalia. Bobby, only a little over four months old, appeared to be taking it all in.

We marched, we milled, we looked over the other cele-
brants. We ate, we lit firecrackers, we visited and gossiped and
listened to speeches and watched a ball game and fireworks. We
competed in races and laughed at floats full of jokesters. We were
all Americans together, celebrating freedom.

Mabel and I sought out our best friends right away. Mother insisted, "Okay, you can have fun, but first you have to listen
to the program. Listen! 'Along the street there comes/ A blare
of bugles, a ruffle of drums.' "

I knew she was quoting from one of her favorite patriotic
poems.

Along Main Street came the Tower-Soudan High School
Band, resplendent in purple and gold uniforms, playing "The
Stars and Stripes Forever." Then the Boy Scouts, the Girl Scouts,
and the veterans of the Spanish-American War and the World
War. Even the Civil War was represented by two old men whose
faded blue eyes took in the scene as if it were old and not very
interesting news.

The parade stopped near the Rex Theater, its marquee
draped with red, white, and blue bunting. The band struck up
"The Star Spangled Banner," and before she joined the singing,

A typical Tower Fourth of July parade, showing a marching band and
streamers across the road.

Mother said, as she always did, "This song just thrills me."

The valedictorian of the Tower-Soudan Class of 1928, looking hot and earnest in a navy blue serge suit, white shirt, and red and blue tie, read the Declaration of Independence from the balcony above the theater entrance. Many of his audience didn't understand all the high-flown language of the Founding Fathers, but they listened as respectfully as if they were attending a religious ceremony.

Every year Dr. Preston Bradley, a Unitarian minister from Chicago who spent summers at his cottage on Lake Vermilion, delivered the oration. He was an old-fashioned spellbinder, his voice and his appearance as magnetic as his words. I thought he looked and sounded as if he'd stepped out of my history book—perhaps as Daniel Webster, with his leonine head of thick graying hair waving back from his high forehead, his sonorous voice, and his rolling phrases. For years he was as much a part of Tower's Fourth as the American flag. Father, a good public speaker himself, took in every word and intonation with unbounded admiration.

Solemnities over, the fun began. We took Bobby to watch the buggy and trike parade of the littlest kids. Some were shy, in need of encouragement from Mom and Dad lest they cry. Others proudly pushed doll buggies and flaunted colonial or ballerina costumes or whatever their mothers' fingers and fancies had created. Little boys stuck out pugnacious chins so no one would laugh at them as they bent over their handlebars and turned as dizzy a spin of red, white, and blue crepe paper as their short legs could produce.

I used Bobby as my excuse for not entering the races for boys and girls of school age—sack races, three-legged races, hundred-yard dashes, carrying eggs in a spoon. Our big brothers counted on winning enough races for the day's spending money, and usually did. Mabel, flushed and proud, won the girls' hundred-yard dash.

When the parade of floats began, Mother came to see if I was tired of holding Bobby. We took turns for a while. We were surprised to hear him laugh out loud at the antics of the grownups. On floats decorated by members of various clubs and employees of local stores, ordinarily staid shopkeepers and housewives and miners cavorted in costume. As always, a man was dressed as a woman with an outrageous blonde wig and grotesquely oversized breasts. As always, a "Chic Sale" outhouse with the traditional crescent on the door betrayed a surprised-looking occupant.

Then came the Indian powwow, the traditional highlight of the day. The Chippewa Indians from the reservation north of the lake were decked out in fringed buckskin garments and beaded moccasins. The men wore long feathered war bonnets and their faces were thickly bedaubed with paint. The women were more modestly dressed in long buckskin robes, simple leather headbands with a jaunty feather stuck in their thick braids, and a few streaks of paint.

When the dancing began, Bobby's sleepiness vanished and he bounced in my arms until I willingly turned him over to Father. Mabel and I were entranced.

Three men sat and beat drums and chanted tribal songs. The others began to shuffle in a circle, and slowly coordinated their steps to the rhythm of the drums. They hopped twice on each foot, then bent way over, picked up speed, straightened up and bent back, brandished their beribboned tomahawks, and challenged the sky with blood-curdling cries.

The women moved more sedately. Several had papooses strapped to boards on their backs; others pulled wide-eyed toddlers along as they shuffled. Only the teen-age girls flouted tradition. They wore modern makeup rather than war paint, and a reluctant air of just going along with the tribe. Mischievous but unsmiling, they occasionally did a few steps of the polka or the Charleston.

The music stopped, and the chief held out a basket for donations as the spectators began to disperse. Mother said she'd take Bobby over to Celia Soper's for lunch and a nap, and we were free to enjoy the rest of the day. With Aili and Bertha, we named one of the braves "Hiawatha" and a girl "Minnehaha," and all the way up Main Street we practiced powwowing for our summer games in the woods.

Until the baseball game began, there was little to do but stroll up and down Main Street, licking ice cream cones or eating hot dogs. Uncles and bachelors and hired men were generous with dimes today. The greatest treat was an ice cream sundae, maybe even a banana split, in Marttila's cool, shady parlor with its tiny marble-topped tables. The four of us postponed that delight until we could wait no longer, and then stretched it out, our sturdy legs wound around the spindly wire ones of the chairs.

Mother didn't let us buy firecrackers. Every Fourth some

child lost an eye or a finger or was badly burned. That didn't deter boys. They threw strings of little firecrackers as near girls' feet as possible and watched them jump and dance with fright. Once in a while a really big firecracker popped, and we blocked our ears. The acrid smell of gunpowder and blue smoke vanishing into the hot summer air mingled with the aromas of coffee, hot dogs, ice cream, and soda pop to create a smell that was pure Fourth of July. We considered buying balloons, but they lasted only a moment before boys popped them. We bought small flags instead on our way to the ball field.

Our brothers insisted on staying for the ball game, and the afternoon stretched interminably. A group of girls lay in the shade of a tree and giggled about the players. When Mabel and I got sleepy we joined Mother at Celia's clean little house, fragrant with coffee and pastries as well as soap and cologne.

Celia told us Mother had one of the headaches that always bothered her on long days away from home, and was lying down in the bedroom with the baby. We curled up foot to foot on the porch swing. We listened a while to the faraway sounds of firecrackers and yelling at the baseball field, and then slept until the game was over and the menfolk came to fetch us.

We would have liked to stay and see the fireworks, but we knew the cows were waiting to be milked, and the older boys had bought fireworks of their own, which they were allowed to set off when the long twilight began to give way to night.

Home felt cool and welcoming. We had left the dark green window shades down and the windows closed, slop pails and garbage emptied, so that only the lingering smell of soap and good food and coffee greeted us. Leo fetched cold lemonade from the spring to rinse away the firecrackery and oversweet tastes of the day.

No one was very hungry after all the unaccustomed treats. But Mother's cool *viili* tasted just right with rhubarb sauce and a slice of whole wheat bread. Mabel sprinkled sugar on her bowl of *viili*. I preferred to scrape off the thick crust and savor each luscious spoonful before I mixed the rhubarb sauce with the yogurt at the bottom.

When Father said it was dark enough, Mabel and I lit our sparklers amid many warnings to be careful and not touch the hot metal after they burned out. We ran around the garden and down the slope of the front yard toward the brook, waved the dazzling golden showers in circles and spirals and sang, "OH, toDAY is the FOURTH of Ju-LY! TODAY is the FOURTH of Ju-LY-EYE!"

Then the boys set up their display; they carefully pointed the rockets away from the house before they lit the fuses. Roman candles and other marvels whooshed into the air and exploded into balls of stars—red, gold, green, blue, and silvery white—and arced down as they faded. Finally, only the stars in the sky were left, and Father said, *"No niin.* Another Forchuly is over."

We all had to wash hands and face and feet, or splash in the cool sauna, before Mother let us go to bed.

"Goodnight, children. Wasn't it a Grand and Glorious Fourth?" she smiled. "But I'm glad to take my Forchuly headache to bed."

Haymaking Time

The powwows and sparklers of the Fourth signaled the end of frolicsome early summer. For many days before that there had been other signs that hot July would bring the serious work of making hay.

Father and the boys sharpened scythes and mower blades on the grindstone at the end of the wagonshed. In his little blacksmith shop by the road, Father hammered out new horseshoes. Mabel and I stood by the door, smelled the burning coal, and waited for the moment when Father plunged the newly-shaped, red-hot iron into a pail of water. The sizzle and smell and heat put us in awe of the power of men. When Father asked us to pump the bellows, we shared in that awesome world.

From hops and other mysterious ingredients, Mother made gallons and gallons of *kaljaa*, a non-alcoholic beer that mellowed in a wooden barrel in the cool *puoji*. Despite the heat, she kept the oven going for coffee breads; there would be twice as many hungry men as usual to feed.

In early summer Mabel and I had often played in the big hayloft over the barn, especially when it was hot or rainy. Only a little hay was left from last summer's crop—just enough to cushion a jump from the swing and to cloud the air with floating golden dust motes highlighted by the sunbeams coming in between the boards of the wall. (Only the downstairs portion of the barn was made of stout logs and concrete.)

Then, a few days before the Fourth, the men opened the hayloft's double doors wide and set long, smooth, silvery-gray poles slanting down to the ground. After that we ignored the ladder and monkey-climbed barefoot up the poles—not to play in the loft, but to slide down, over and over again.

Haymaking began on the fifth of July, and for three weeks or so it was the main purpose of existence. To be sure of milk and cream and butter the rest of the year, we had to fill lofts and haymows with sun-dried fodder for the cows. The team of horses that hauled the hay and firewood also had to have their share. Hay was worth every sunburn, insect bite, aching muscle, and mad race against rainstorms. It was the time of greatest cooperation and highest drama, and Mabel and I played strong supporting roles. Despite the heat and work, we loved it.

Early on the morning of the fifth, Father took Mabel with him to Virginia, where he knew itinerant workmen would be

The cream separator, the wringer washer with Father's winter boots on top, scythes, harness and other farm equipment.

sitting on their packsacks or standing in little knots in the shade of Temperance Hall, waiting for farmers to come and hire them for haying.

Since very early morning Victor had been leading the other haymakers swinging their scythes in low-lying meadows and along the margins of the brooks where the horse-drawn mower couldn't go. Father had taught him not only to sharpen all the needed tools but also to swing the scythe. Each evening he told Vic where to cut and take the lead swath and work "like hell" to set the pace for the others. They started early because the thick tall grass was easier to cut while dew still lay on it. The whining whap-whap of whetstones sharpening scythe blades rang now from one direction, now from another. Before breakfast, they had worked about three hours in the heavy, dew-wet grass.

By 1928 Father had a horse-drawn mower for the drier fields. That July fifth, when they heard the Ford arrive in mid-morning, the haymakers came for coffee, curious to see whom Father had picked up in town. He was Otto Niemi, the same neat, brush-cut bachelor who had already worked on the farm for several summers and returned for winter tasks. He had virtually become part of the household. Mabel confided, "He teased me all the way home that the new baby would be his pet now, not me anymore. But I don't believe him. He just likes to tease."

As always, Matt pedaled his bicycle over early every morning to help. Mother didn't mind his smell so much when he spent most of the time outdoors, had a sauna every night and went home early to sleep.

As always, Uncles Ray and Felix could be counted on, especially when they were on night shift in the mine, to help save a crop when rain threatened, or before it became so dry that it crumbled if not quickly packed into haylofts and stacks. In turn, the boys helped them make hay on Grandpa's farm, four miles away.

Father was the star of the drama, king of the green and gold domain of hay. He rode the mower behind Billy and Jimmy, our reddish-brown, knobby-kneed, short-legged work horses. He maneuvered the handle that lowered the wicked upright shaft to just the right level—low enough so that the glistening blades would flash against each other and cut the hay into wide swaths, but not so low as to hit stones and nick a carefully-sharpened edge. Then he clicked his tongue, shook the reins smartly, and said, "Giddyap!" and the horses bent their necks, strained at the creak-

Father with his hard-working team, Billy and Jimmy.

ing harness, and pulled the mower clacking and clattering round and round the fields of timothy, clover, and alfalfa.

Mabel and I always wanted to be there when this happened. The smell of new-mown hay intoxicated us. We squealed at the abundant and panic-stricken animals that tried to escape the invading monster. Grasshoppers leaped madly. Mice scurried, abandoning curled-up bundles of squirming pink babies. Birds squawked up from hidden nests, which we looked for so we could try to save the babies. We jumped when an occasional harmless garter snake wriggled away into uncut grass. We watched hawks wheeling in the sky, alert for easy prey.

After Father had circled the first field a few times, we brought him coffee. He took off his visored cotton cap and wiped his forehead with the red bandanna he wore around his neck. We knew from the way he squinted at the spiralling rows of new-cut hay and smiled at us that all was going well—so far.

For mowers sometimes broke down, and parts had to be improvised or fetched from town. Every moment was precious. If rain came, hay could spoil. If it weren't cut in time, it could turn to brittle dust in the hot sun. Father had to watch the fields and decide just when to cut a certain one, and when to change from the mower to the one-horse rake, stepping on the lever every few minutes to lift the curved comb of enormous tines and leave a wide row to dry. At each stage he tested the hay and studied the weather signs. He bent stalks of uncut hay or crushed handfuls of drying hay and gazed at the summer sky. Then he decided if it was time for the mower, time to turn the rows of hay to dry in the sun, time to load the wagon or sleigh and take it to the hayloft or pile it into stacks.

Boys, uncles, and hired men were busy in the fields meanwhile, raking, swinging their scythes where the mower couldn't go, building small stacks.

The stable and puoji.

With the baby to tend as well as cooking, washing, milking, and gardening, Mother worked even longer hours than the men. She made Mabel and me feel more important than ever and often said, "I just don't know what I'd do without you. Your legs are so much younger than mine." We did a hundred helpful little chores, often without being asked, and if we ever complained, I don't remember it now.

We rose early, and by the time we went to bed fresh from sauna, we had run and run and run and run, hither and yon. We had carried lard pails full of hot coffee rich with cream and sugar, which the men slurped thirstily from tin cups while they emptied brown paper bags of Mother's baked goods—cookies, cinnamon buns, butterscotch-pecan rolls, blueberry muffins, biscuits. In emergencies, when she hadn't had time to bake, the men had to be content with *korppuja*.

Several times a day we answered a call for cold drinks. We lifted the two-quart jars of *kaljaa* or root beer from the cold spring in the brook, where they dangled from lengths of twine. We drank generously from the spigot as we refilled the jars from the barrels in the shed. We seldom had time to stop at the log bridge over the brook by the sauna to watch the dragonflies and water skeeters.

The washing of dishes and clothes was endless. But at least the clothes dried quickly in summer, and the men's blue chambray shirts and bib overalls could do without ironing, while the boys went shirtless, bragged about how brown they were getting, and compared their biceps after a few days of haying.

It was the cooking—breakfast, two big meals, and two coffees, with perhaps a third in the evening, that kept Mother so extra busy. Mabel and I hunted through the garden for new young carrots, cut rhubarb for pies, fetched flour from the shed and potatoes, cabbages, rutabagas, carrots, and beets from the root cellar, and dug new potatoes for my favorite food, Mother's delicious potato and onion soup, rich with milk and butter. We peeled and chopped and stirred, peeked in the oven to see if the bread was done, ran for an emergency "lap" of firewood. At dinner time we filled a colander with leaf lettuce, washed it at the spring, shook it dry, and mixed sweet cream, a sprinkle of sugar, and a dollop of mustard for dressing. We set the table with a small extra plate of butter at Matt's place—Mother's solution after she despaired of convincing him not to help himself from the butter dish after he had licked his knife.

At the end of each day Father called a halt, and the weary workmen went first to the sauna to wash off dust and sweat and prickly bits of hay. When the sauna was cooler, Mabel and I took Bobby there; he sat up in a tub by now and splashed merrily. Mother preferred to wait until after milking and supper time so she could have a long leisurely bath alone.

Often, especially on very hot days, we piled into the car at noon before eating dinner, and perhaps again at sunset, and drove to Grandpa's lake for a cooling skinny dip. Mabel and I yelled for the men to hurry up, and raced down, wrapped in towels, through the damp moss and swamp laurel flagged with wild blue

Grandpa's lake.

iris. Sometimes we had a bath first in Grandpa's old *savusauna*, black with layers of soot because there was no chimney for the smoke to escape through. An occasional city visitor hung back, sure she would come out pitch black, but the satiny black didn't stick to the skin.

When rain threatened, even Mabel and I were called to help with the haying. If Mother could spare time from the house and baby, she came too, and everyone furiously raked the cut hay into rows and then piled it into stacks. If the wagon couldn't get it to the barn before the heavens opened up, at least it would stay drier inside a stack, and we could spread it out again when the sun shone.

Sliding a load of hay up the long silvery poles into the barn loft was the climax of the haying drama. To ensure a smooth ride, the sleigh had to be heaped just right. One man on top packed down the hay that the others pitched up forkful after forkful from the small stacks. Vic and Ray vied for the honor of being good load makers, as Father had taught them. I thought they looked like Greek gods as they stood higher and higher on the load, bare bronzed arms rippling with muscle, hair bleached gold by the sun.

Leo's round face beamed with pride as he rode one of the horses to the barn. When he had his fill of glory, he might let Mabel have the honor, but I was afraid of the horses and preferred to watch.

The load stopped at the foot of the slanted poles, and a workman, standing in the hayloft, fed out the hayfork on a pulley cable. The flat-topped A-shaped metal fork was designed with a double bar across it near the top, and two movable prongs at the bottom to grasp the hay. The man atop the load worked it down into what he hoped was the critical center of a well-built load, and pulled on the levers that tightened the prongs to grip that spot. If he was right, the whole load slid up the poles in one neat beautiful package.

While he worked with the fork, others unhitched the team and drove it around to the back of the barn. There they fastened the other end of the cable, which emerged from a small opening high in the wall, down to the pulleys and the harness below.

A shout of "Aw righ!" told the men in front that the team was ready, and the load maker jumped clear. I squeezed my arms tight across my chest in suspense when Father yelled, "OK, Go het!" and the horses strained to pull the hay in one smooth effort up the poles and through the wide door into the loft. Usually all but a few wisps of hay made it. If not, they rebuilt the now ragged load and tried again. One man stayed in the loft to spread the hay while the others—after long rewarding swallows of *kaljaa* from the nearby spring—went back to the fields for more.

It was easier, if not as exciting, to fill the three haymows out in the meadow—log cabins with outward-slanting walls and tin roofs. Or, if the crop was abundant, the men built beehive-shaped stacks with canvas covers around central supporting poles. Those jobs done, haymaking time was over for another year.

Bears and Blueberries

"Why can't there be a vacation between haymaking and blueberry picking?" Leo was crazy about baseball and softball, and he felt cheated of them both during July. The warm summer and ample rain had plumped and ripened the berries even before the hay was in. Already each member of the family, on other comings and goings, had spotted good patches. Already Mabel and I had gone out with five-pound lard pails to pick enough for muffins or pancakes, and even for several pies.

But a couple of days of heavy rain ruled out both ball games and blueberry picking. While thunder rumbled through the hills, I found the book Mother had taken from me when I was churning—*The Vanishing American*, by Zane Grey.

All day long I read, lost in the story of Indians dispossessed of ancient tribal lands and forests, water sources, buffalo herds, and trapping areas. My head began to ache in the dim light, but I read on. At coffee time Mother came upstairs and found me tossing, feverish, on the bed, my head aching intolerably. She was able to make no sense of what I said—something about "Oh, how cruel! Oh, the poor Indians!"—until she saw the thick red book beside me. She took me down to her own cool bedroom, laid damp cloths wrung out of vinegar water on my forehead, and gave me one of the powders an itinerant peddler had sold her, which had cured many of her own headaches. The storm cleared. My delirium left me and I slept.

When I woke up, Vic was sitting on the sofa, fresh from sauna, hair slicked back, dressed for a dance in white shirt and tie. "Hey, little *sisko*, I was worried about you. That Western really upset you."

I nodded groggily. "It's not just an ordinary Western; it tells how badly the whites treated the Indians, and pushed them off their own land."

"You could say we did that around here too. All this was Chippewa territory. You can find injustice almost anywhere. The mine owners, the lumber barons. . . . .But don't you get sick worrying about it. Some day I'll try to change all that, but you are just a smart little kid who should be having fun and not just studying and reading all the time. Grow up a lot more and maybe get to be a teacher before you worry too much about the world's problems."

"But you're only fourteen and you go to workers' meetings and you read a lot of things about world revolution and argue politics and scary stuff. . ."

"Never mind. I am different. That is the only way I can change anything in this world. But your motto is *'ei kun paljo'* and maybe your way of helping others means you have to help yourself get ahead first. You know how to have fun and enjoy life; don't change that. I'd hate to think you're sad here after I leave home."

Leave home! I'd never thought of that before. Home meant all of us together, forever. Even though I wanted to go away, and travel, somehow home had to stay the same.

"Oh, Vic, don't talk like that," I wailed. "You're too young. And you're the only one I can really talk to—the only one who really listens to me. Don't go." I wiped my eyes on the damp pillowcase.

Vic patted my shoulder and said cheerfully, "I'm not going anywhere yet, just to a barn dance. Father let me have the car tonight because it's not that far and the haymaking is done. Come have supper. You know the sun's shining again and the whole gang goes blueberry picking tomorrow."

At midnight on New Year's Eve, Mother had gone out to look at the sky. "It's full of stars. This will be a good blueberry year," she announced, with complete faith in her systems of omens.

She was happy to be proven right. At the edges of the forests, and in clearings where young trees and bushes gave shade, the stiff sturdy blueberry plants were heavy with fruit. For weeks, we had watched the clusters of waxy pinkish-green bells turn a deeper pink, and then a silver-misted blue. Now on our first day of serious berrying, Mother and the five older kids left Father to find out what it was like to take care of a five-month-old for a few hours, and took off for the woods beyond the common pasture, carrying pails of all sizes.

"Pick clean now, and pick into the pail," Mother reminded us. "Every berry you eat now is one less for winter, and you know how you like them on pancakes and rice pudding, not to mention in pies and muffins."

Mother stopped where outcroppings of glacial rock were overhung with low bushes thick with berries. I spotted clusters of huge blue berries misted with a silver sheen, and was about to call out, "Hey, here's some as big as grapes," when I thought better of it and kept the patch to myself. But Mother said, "Goodness gracious, these berries are almost as big as grapes," and I felt less selfish.

For a while everyone picked silently. We tried to avoid picking leaves, twigs, shriveled berries, and pink or green ones that would ripen in another week or two. We swiped at flies and gnats, stepped carefully around soft marshy places and holes where we might twist an ankle, and dead-looking branches that might still have enough life in them to give us a whack if we trod on one end. We drank lemonade from the thermos, and once in a while we sneaked farther off into the bushes to relieve ourselves behind a wide tree trunk. Each of us looked for a solid mossy rock in the shade, with berries in all directions.

When I stood up to stretch, I looked around and laughed. Mother was bending over, just as she did in the garden. Mabel knelt on her folded sweater. Ray was squatting, pail between his knees, as if he were milking the berries. Vic was wandering from patch to patch, grabbing handfuls here and there. Leo had found a hole to stand in, with the bushes level with his waist; he had tied the pail to his waist with a piece of twine so he could use both hands.

I emptied my lard pail into one of the big milk pails, and was glad to see that it was more than half full already. Suddenly Mother said, "I think I know an even better place; come on, I'm tired of this one."

She shooed us nearer an open clearing. She look so worried and bustled along so fast that I ran to catch up, and asked, "What's the matter? Did you see a snake?"

"No, I did *not* see a snake. Come on, let's sing."

Before we got very far along in our discordant chorus of "My Old Kentucky Home," another promising patch was in sight. In another hour every receptacle was full, and we turned homeward.

Father was very glad to see us. He had sat Bobby on his knee, held his hands, and bounced him while he recited, *"Körön körön kirkko,"* and Bobby was so delighted with the new game that Father tired of it long before the baby did.

"I have soup waiting," Mother said, "and we can't take time for real naps. Just stretch out in the shade for a while and then start picking over the berries before they settle and get wet and it will be just that much harder to pick them clean."

We knew she was right, but cleaning was a long, slow, boring job. We tried various methods to speed it up. We tossed berries from one hand to the other, blew away the leaves, spread the berries on a clean dishtowel or newspaper on the grass in the shade of the pine trees, and counted berries as we worked. The day was so warm we had to talk and laugh just to stay awake.

Ray's wit helped. "You know blueberries are what keep us going all winter, don't you?" he asked solemnly.

"Yeah," I said, "but there's potatoes, too, and deer meat, and the vegetables Mother cans, and bread. . . "

"No, dummy, I mean keep you *going*—to the outhouse!"

When the smell of coffee overpowered that of blueberries, which by now had cloyed, we rose to go to the house. I went in first and overheard Mother telling Father she had seen a huge black bear, but hadn't told us for fear we might panic.

"Mother, is that true? Why didn't you tell us? It would have been fun to see a real black bear in the woods."

Ray scoffed. "Look who's talking. You'd have been the first to turn tail and run. The bear was probably happy just eating berries. Bears don't usually attack unless they're afraid for their cubs. If it had seen us it would have probably just lumbered away in the opposite direction."

He bent over, hands curled into paws on the floor, and did a slow, ambling imitation of a bear looking this way and that as it shuffled away, sniffing for honey or berries.

"I think Mother was very brave not to tell us. She was defending her cubs, too," said Mabel.

From then on, through the rest of berry season, we were all watchful; no one wanted to frighten a bear or be frightened by one.

For weeks I had dreamed of hay in rows and stacks and wagonloads and dramatic swoops into the hayloft. Now I saw thousands of big blue berries, hanging as temptingly as bunches of grapes among their stiff little green leaves passing across the screen of my dreams as I turned in sleep to ease my tired body.

Summer's End

On July 27 I opened my eyes to bright sunshine and jumped out of bed. Today I was nine!

While I dressed, I sniffed the rich aroma of deer liver baking with onions, a sure sign that Father had killed his first deer of the season during the night. Not, of course, the legal deer-hunting season, but the first time since winter that bucks were fat enough for the kill.

Relatives and friends shared summer meat because it could spoil. We kept our share fresh in wooden barrels of heavy brine sunk to water level in the icy cold muskeg of the black spruce swamp beyond the little hill, safe from the game warden's searches. Not that wardens were very zealous. They knew that deer had become so abundant since much of the land was cleared that they even browsed in garden plots, and that the farmers needed the meat for their families.

While Mother and I picked my birthday bouquet of deep blue delphiniums heavy with dew, we decided on a chocolate cake with seven-minute frosting; of course I would get to lick the bowl. Mother promised, "I'll ask Father to let you off picking

79

potato bugs until tomorrow. That's not a very nice job for a birthday girl. But you've got to pick blueberries and pull a few weeds."

The ordeal of birthday wishes from the menfolks lasted until each had appeared and spanked me nine times, with a tenth to grow on. "And not just sideways, with all that potato soup you eat," said Ray.

Mabel chattered cheerfully while we knelt on mossy rocks near the little hill and picked berries. But I didn't really listen. I pondered the mystery of being born and growing up to have one birthday after another. Mother told me the same story on every birthday: "After four boys I wanted a girl so badly that I nearly jumped out of bed with joy when you were born—it was 3:30 Sunday morning, and you've been an early bird ever since." Even the thought of the fourth boy, who had lived only six weeks, couldn't cloud this bright day. I remembered the verse Mother had recited when Bobby first opened his eyes and looked around at all of us:

Where did you come from, baby dear?
Out of the everywhere into the here.
Where did you get those eyes so blue?
Out of the sky as I came through.

By now I had caught on to the astonishing idea that babies grew inside her. Still, her answers to my questions about growing old and dying were not at all satisfactory. She only talked about being saved and going to Heaven, or, when she had listened to some fiery preacher, about the end of the world, when everyone would go to either Heaven or Hell. These answers left me uncomfortable and unsatisfied. Grandpa was the oldest person I knew. Maybe he could tell me—well, something.

Grandpa, Uncles Ray and Felix, and Aunt Hilma appeared at coffee time, each with a present—candy from the uncles, a blue voile dress with white lace collar from Hilma's clever fingers, and a wriggly rubber fishing lure from Grandpa, who knew how I hated to handle minnows and worms.

"I think the fish will be biting tonight," twinkled Grandpa. "Come over after supper and I'll take you out in the boat and we'll try your birthday luck. You too, of course, *Meiboli*," he added when he saw Mabel's pleading look.

Just before sunset Grandpa rowed his wooden boat almost as far as the tiny island in the middle of the lake. I gazed at the shimmering reflections of pines and birches along the margins of the lake and dabbled a hand in the cool water. I tried to reach one of the yellow water lilies that looked like buds reluctant to open all the way. I thought the wide-open look of the white ones was much nicer, and I plucked one as we floated through the lily pads, and looked deep into its creamy face.

The island's reedy shore was thick with long brown plushy cattails. Only three small balsam pines and two slender birches grew on the little scrap of land.

Grandpa had taught us to be quiet so we wouldn't disturb the fish, but I asked softly, "Grandpa, tell us about Grandma. Mother says she was fat and jolly and died when she was 36, leaving eight kids. But I want to know what she was like when she was young."

Grandpa cleared his throat, spat into the clear water, and settled his mind to the topic.

"*No niin*. I was a young man from Finland and I'd worked in the copper mines and logging camps in Michigan, and survived a typhoid epidemic. My mother wouldn't come to *Ameriika* because she heard about so many troubles here, and my father went back after a couple of years. That summer—it was 1893" —here Mabel and I looked at each other wide-eyed—"I worked as a farmhand at *Meeri*'s parents' farm near New York Mills, because my father worked nearby."

"*Meeri* had come from Finland with her parents when she was just about your age, but by then she was nineteen and worked as a waitress at Yellowstone Park. So I didn't see her all summer.

"*No niin*. One evening in August they asked me to meet her at the train the next day. That night I saw her in a dream, so rosy-cheeked and pretty and lively. I knew her the minute she stepped off the train. She was the girl in my dream, even to the clothes she was wearing. I never again thought of going back to Finland."

Grandpa came out of his reverie with a laugh and said, "This is no way to catch fish. Let's see if we can be quiet for ten minutes. The mosquitoes are getting bad." But only the mosquitoes were biting that evening, and soon he rowed back to shore. I thought about what he had said, but even that only made me wonder more about living and dying.

On the way home from Grandpa's Father sang "*Alasti Synnyin*," his favorite wandering boy song:

Grandpa's home on the lake, October, 1910. Grandpa (Jacob Lempia) with his team; Grandma holding Hilma, Richard, Helen, Pearl, Hilja and Ray. The ladder leaning against the house was not left there by accident. Chim-

ney fires were a constant threat in houses of this era. The ladder allowed easy and quick access to the roof in an effort to put them out. The house did burn down in 1925.

Naked was I born into the lap of the world,
And started my days with a cry.
I know the place where I was born,
And where I played with my little brothers and sisters,
Eating my bread without any anxiety.
The foxes have their dens and the birds their nests,
And the bears their homes in the forest.
Only the wandering boy, winter and summer,
Joyously sings and is free of care.

When we reached the far gate and Mabel jumped out to open it, Father said, "There the home place still stands." He always said this, partly to tease Mother and partly to reassure her. Ever since her old home—the big house Grandpa built as soon as possible after they moved to the farm—burned down one hot windy Sunday afternoon in 1925, she had feared fire.

The house looked like a face; the upstairs windows were the eyes, closed tonight in the dark. Starlight outlined the pines behind the house like an abundant head of hair. The kitchen windows smiled a welcome, and I knew the boys were back from their ball game.

The Lempia family in 1901. Lydia, 5; Jacob, 33; Helen, 4 months; Mary, 27; Hilja (my mother), 7; and Richard, 2.

In bed that night I pondered again the mysteries of being born, and growing, and getting old, and dying whether young or old. Of being born in one country and moving across an ocean to another where they spoke a different language. I tried to picture my Grandma Mary at my age, soon after she had come from Finland. How bewildered she must have been! It was hard enough to understand the grown-up world even when you knew the language. Father, for example. He sang those melancholy orphan boy and wanderer songs, yet he sounded happy to get home from a visit and see the house smiling a welcome.

Then I imagined the pretty girl who met Grandpa when he was a handsome young man, and married him and had eight children. And now he was wrinkled and nearly bald and a little stooped. And Grandma died at 36, and Mother was 34. . .and now I was nine and . . .how long would we all live?

Then I thought of my pretty new dress and the good birthday cake, the sunny day, and sunset on Grandpa's beautiful little lake, and how much everyone in the family loved me. Pleasures and surprises beckoned me far into an unending future.

Next day Father sent Mabel and me to the potato field, each with a coffee can with a half an inch of kerosene in the bottom, to the hated task of picking potato bugs. The field was pretty; white flowers blossomed on all the low-growing dark green plants. We knelt between the rows and looked for the orange-and-black striped beetles that would ruin the potato crop if we allowed them to chew the leaves, and dropped each greedy bug into the can.

After a while I confessed my worries of the night before, and at the same time sought comfort for us both. "Mother won't die when she's 36 just because her mother did. It was January and they had no car, and her appendix burst and they didn't know much about operations, so she died. Now they know, and we have a car, and anyway only old people die nowadays."

"How about our cousin, Billy Lehto?" Mabel said. "He was only 17."

I thought of the studio portrait of the handsome boy asleep in white satin banked with flowers, and said, "Oh, but he was very wild and rode a motorcycle and had an accident. Mother and Father won't let any of us do that."

"And she says if people have been good they go to Heaven when they die and are happy there, but if they've been bad they go to Hell."

Mabel put down her coffee can and mimicked Andrew Kahtava on a binge—"in Russian church," as the Finns called drunkenness—telling old stories in his high falsetto voice. I acted out his solemn taking of the Temperance pledge, and his sudden fall, and the hiccups and staggering that followed. Then we tried to outdo each other imitating the ranting of Isaac Wirtala, a self-styled preacher Mother sometimes took us to hear. We roared in the deepest voices we could muster, "You will all burn in Hell unless you repent and give up your evil ways." In Finnish, out in the sunny field, the words sounded only a distant echo of damnation, and we laughed so hard we sat down in the dusty furrow to catch our breaths before any more bugs met their fate.

❧❧❧❧❧❧❧❧❧❧❧❧

A few days later, the bugs nearly conquered, we heard Mother calling, "Gurr-rulls! Come home now!" The mail had brought a letter from Uncle Arvid and Aunt Hulda. They would drive from Minneapolis and arrive on Sunday afternoon for their usual summer visit.

"Help me finish canning these berries," Mother said, "and then we have to clean. This morning my upper lip itched like crazy, and I knew company was coming."

Mason and Bell jars boiled in one huge kettle, purple blueberry sauce in another. After Mother filled each jar we put on the rubber-lined lid and then screwed the ring on loosely; we tightened it only after the jars had cooled. Purple stains and splashes had to be wiped away. "That makes 64 quarts so far. And there's plenty more in the woods."

Curtains came down and rag rugs came off the floors to be washed, dishes out of cupboards so that new shelf paper could be put down. When the white curtains were blowing on the line, Mother scrubbed the outhouse and sprinkled lime into each of the two lidded holes, put down a clean old rag rug, and added "real toilet paper" to the Co-op shopping list. She polished the big cast-iron range with stove blacking until it shone. Ray hung fresh spirals of sticky yellow flypaper from the ceilings. Vic drove back and forth on errands. Leo scrubbed the sauna.

Mabel and I did all our usual chores, but with special urgency and care, because Arvid and Hulda were so very neat and clean. I washed the lamp chimneys in water with a few drops of kerosene added, and dried them with old newspapers; my hands were still small enough to reach inside and turn the paper round and round until each chimney gleamed. I trimmed the wicks and filled the lamps carefully from the red gallon can of kerosene. Mabel climbed on a chair to get down the big tin match box from the wall by the stove and refill it with wooden kitchen matches. We ran to the shed for flour, stirred cake dough in the big yellow crockery bowl with the blue and white striped band around it, carried firewood, and washed dishes.

Between chores we took Bobby out into the shade of the pines and brushed away flies while he cooed and kicked on a rug. And—at ages nine and six—we reminisced. The content has changed over the years; the pattern of our talk is, perhaps, not very different:

"'Member last summer," said Mabel, "when we drove down to Minneapolis with Father and Mother, and it rained so much we had to stop three times to put up the side curtains?"

"Yeah, and you were scared of the thunder and lightning."

"Go jump in the lake! So were you!"

"And Uncle Arvid's house had such soft chairs and a red plush sofa, and those lacy things Aunt Hulda made on the arms and backs, and a big radio, and a 'frigerator. And she's such a good cook."

"Yeah, but not as good as Mother. And they're rich, and they can buy stuff in Minneapolis that we can't get here."

"And when we drove downtown there were such big bright lights on the theaters, moving and blinking, and they took us to see 'Stella Dallas,' and you cried and cried."

"So what! You did too!"

"And Uncle Arvid showed us his barber shop, and it smelled so good and was so clean. Not like Charlie Niemi's bachelor camp."

We were giggling again when Mother reminded us that it was late and the curtains were still not up, and she needed help getting them on the rods.

Saturday was cream day as usual. When Mother and Father left for town, Mabel rode as far as the mailbox and ran home with the Sunday *Duluth Herald*, with its page after page of brightly-colored funnies. We lay on our stomachs on the clean rag rugs

Uncle Arvid in his Chevrolet, 1930. Mother, crouched with Bobby, Mabel, Leo and Mavis.

in the cool bedroom. Mabel first read her favorite, "The Katzenjammer Kids," and I turned to "Bringing Up Father," enjoying the antics of Maggie with her rolling pin and Jiggs with his paunch and brush cut.

Soon Vic came in and said, "Hey, girls, Orphan Annie can wait till after sauna tonight. Maw wants you to pick some berries for pies and have them all cleaned when she gets back."

I opened my mouth to whine, "I'm only eight and I have to work like a mule," when I remembered that I was nine, and that Mother had told us how she worked when she was nine. They lived in Virginia then, and Grandma kept twenty boarders who worked in the new open-pit iron mines, and cooked for them and washed their rust-red clothes. She also kept cows and was famed for her sweet butter and clean milk. Sometimes Mother woke in the night and found her bent over the washtub, crying with weariness. She would turn the wringer for her mother, and folded clothes from the line the next day.

But Grandma was never really sorry for herself, and was jolly, and laughed, and sang, Mother told us, and was very sociable. She enjoyed the coffee socials with her friends at Temperance Hall. We got the idea that it would be a good thing if we grew up to be like her.

While we cleaned the berries, we played a guessing game about what our aunt and uncle would bring us this time. They always brought something old, something new, something nice, and something horrid. Always candy. And always something useful.

The next morning, Mother made *juustoa*—pressed fresh cheese made with rennet and baked in the oven until it was mottled a soft golden brown. As a special treat we were allowed to dip slices of *juustoa* in coffee until it was soft and warm and squeaked when we bit into it.

Long before the visitors could be expected, we kept looking out the window and down the road. In midafternoon a car finally turned in at the far gate, trailing a cloud of dust. Mabel won our usual race to be the first to call out, "Car coming!"

The car drove up to the front steps with a flourish. Uncle Arvid was showing off a new black Chevrolet with glass windows that rolled up and down rather than side curtains.

The visitors emerged, pink, round, and smiling, from their chariot. We ran to embrace Aunt Hulda's softness; her bosom was like a warm pillow. Her smile, framed by a ruffled dust cap, was full of love for her husband's nieces and nephews. As always, Uncle Arvid wore a straw hat and a white shirt, a bit sweaty from the long drive. His balding pate was traced with a few dark strands combed from one side over to the other. He peered at the family through his rimless glasses and said, "First I want a drink of the best water in the world," and headed for the pail of drinking water in the kitchen. He swallowed three dippersful, and exhaled a long sigh of satisfaction after each one.

Hulda wanted to see the baby, and when Uncle Arvid wasn't listening, she said, "Oh, lucky you, Hilja, to have children to love and comfort you."

In the kitchen, meanwhile, Uncle Arvid was pontificating to his older brother about the folly of bringing so many children into a family already crowding the little house and demanding food, clothes, and all sorts of foolishness they had never had as children. He asked the boys to heat the sauna, and they assured him it had been warming for an hour.

Uncle Arvid asked to see our report cards, complimented us, and then spoiled our pleasure by saying, "It won't be long before you can get a job sewing at Munsingwear and repay your parents for raising you." Aunt Hulda had a job there, but it was certainly not my idea of *ei kun paljo*—of the American dream that Superintendent Barnes had promised. She was happy with it, because she knew very little English, and it earned her much more money than she would have made in Finland. But quite aside from my clumsiness—I once sewed right through my finger with the school machine—it was a far cry from my dreams of teaching, writing, and travel.

The boxes we had been waiting for soon appeared. We were embarrassed by the horrid used clothes Aunt Hulda had seen fit to collect for us. But there were new bloomers and stockings too, a new dress for each of us, and a bag of candy corn and yellowish banana-shaped marshmallows. When Mother served coffee, we retreated to the stairs to eat candy and listen.

The visitors had recently returned from a trip to Finland, and were eager to tell all about it.

"You know," said Uncle Arvid, "we always thought we'd go back some day after we became rich in the golden land, but there's nothing for us there. They're all just about as poor as when we left. No one has a car or a phone.

"Of course, *Suomi* is free now and boys don't have to worry about being drafted into the Russian army, but *Ameriika* is much better. Our brothers still live in the old houses by the lake. Kaisa and Liisa died in childbirth. The land is poor. They thought we were rich beyond their wildest dreams of anything they could achieve in Finland."

To Mabel and me, too, Arvid was our rich uncle. He had a house with a furnace and indoor toilet and running water and electricity, and he loaned Father money when he needed it, although he always preached a little sermon along with the loan. But we did have a phone and a car, and good schools. And Vic and I, at least, hoped to go to college some day.

When the conversation turned to people we'd never heard of, we lost interest and went out to the front steps. Soon Uncle Arvid came out and said, "Hey, girls, your hair's too long. Get a chair and I'll cut it out here in the yard."

Mabel ran away a few yards, turned around, and yelled, "Don't you dare give me a boyish bob this time!" He had surprised her with one in Minneapolis, and she had cried and kicked and screamed, and even hit her beloved uncle, who finally pacified her by showing her pictures to prove it was the latest style.

Now he snipped lightly and deftly, but we shivered when he had us bend our heads so he could run the clippers over the back of the neck. Then he brushed our necks with a silky-soft brush, shook out the towel, and held up a mirror so we could admire our newly-neat Dutch bobs. "I'll get the boys tomorrow," he said with a wink.

While Aunt Hulda helped Mother with supper, and the boys, for a change, milked the cows, Mabel and I had to show off our strength and dexterity to Uncle Arvid. Mabel hooked her fingers over the lintel of the door between the two rooms and hung there for over a minute. Flexible but not as strong, I tucked both legs behind my neck. He gave us each a dime. He tested the boy's biceps, too, and pronounced, "Soon your father won't have to pay any hired men; he'll have three good farm workers."

The week was busy with visits to and from their *omanpaikkaset*, blueberry picking, fishing in Grandpa's lake, saunas, naps, and talk, talk, talk. I had heard people say the Finns weren't talkers, and thought, they should be around when relatives and *omanpaikkeset* get together!

The men were rosy and damp from Saturday night sauna. Ray and Vic appeared in newly pressed pants and white shirts and ties. "Where are these young *herrat* going?" Uncle Arvid asked, incredulous. Father explained that they had been very good workers during haymaking time, and that they were going to a dance at Vermilion Hall, only three miles away.

"But they haven't even finished *rippikoulu*; and it's not the same as when we were young and went to dances on skis or by riverboat." He shook his head in disapproval. No one told him how rare this privilege was, and how often the boys pleaded in vain to go anywhere on Saturday night.

Early next morning Uncle Arvid and Uncle Hulda left, promising to return in November for deer-hunting season. As the Chevrolet pulled away, Mother collapsed into the rocking chair, pushed out her teeth, and said, "Thank goodness that's over."

Our laughter was sincere, but changed to fake groans when Mother began to list all the work that had to be done before school began.

"Lots more blueberries. Beet pickles, dill pickles, carrot pickles, piccalilli, chow chow, relish. Jam and jelly—blueberry, raspberry, maybe plum if Ray finds some in the woods. Canned green beans and carrots, and some stew for Ray to take to high school when he is batching it. Oh, and maybe Father will buy me a couple of crates of peaches and pears. I'm so glad I've got two good helpers."

We heard a wail from the bedroom. She felt her dress, wet at the breasts, and went to nurse the baby. We ran outside to savor a moment of freedom from dear but demanding relatives and boring and endless chores.

On the hillside behind the chicken coop we found that the dark chokecherries that puckered our mouths were ripe; Mother would want those to make delicious jelly. We gorged on the ripe purple berries that grew separately on head-high bushes and for want of a more accurate name we called them sugar plums. Between handfuls of sweetness we tucked our chins in our chests and imitated Arvid's low-voiced manner of giving well-meant advice: "I'm telling you this for your own good—and, of course, I live in a big city and I know."

Soon, however, the voice from down the hill grew more insistent: "Gur-ruls! Come on home. I have to milk the cows and you have to watch the baby and wash the breakfast dishes." We ran out of the woods, past the chicken coop, and through the field of dry grass behind the wagonshed. We stopped only a minute to pluck black-eyed Susans, soft blue chicory, and Queen Anne's Lace for a bouquet.

When most of the canning was done, and the first day of school drew near, Mother gave each of us a length of flowered cotton, blue for Mabel, green for me, to take to Alma Simonson, who stitched up neat shirtdresses just alike. Aili Juntunen lived nearby, and we stole a few minutes for a visit with her each time we went for a fitting.

On each walk to her house we saw more signs that summer was ending. Goldenrod and pearly everlasting were in bloom. Everywhere in the cutover land and along the roadsides the purple-pink spikes of fireweed flamed. Here and there a maple branch already flared bright red, promised even greater beauty, and signaled the approach of winter.

Although the promise of eternal summer was broken, we looked forward to the day after Labor Day, when we would wear our "first day of school dresses." But we had missed other signals that foretold autumnal gloom at home.

Am I right in thinking of that summer of 1928 as the last truly happy and carefree one of my childhood? I am sure that from then on many of the things I learned were learned at the price of tears. I sometimes wept when Father's idea of meikäläiset—*our kind of people, which I translated at age nine as "poor farmers"— clashed with Mother's ideals of Americanization and her hopes for her children, and with my own wishes. And when adult mysteries guarded like terrible secrets turned out, I thought, not to be terrible at all. And when death was made more terrifying by fanatical preaching about sin and salvation. Most of all, I wept over the pain of watching a beloved brother pulling away from the rest of the family—his hopes thwarted by poverty and rigid old ideas, which turned him toward the promises preached by new and alien ones. Ideological battles tore our family apart, just as they disrupted the Finnish community in the years when the Depression began, before it was called "The Great."*

But those years were by no means all gloom and dreariness. I still played the clown, danced—alone in the woods or at parties at Vermilion Hall or School 40—till I was out of breath, studied hard, read voraciously, and ate Mother's wonderful food as if I knew food would never again taste quite so good.

If I had a motto, it was still ei kun paljo. *Life offered a great array of wonderful possibilities, and I was sure some of them would come my way. Yet after that Labor Day of 1928, I was never again quite so freely and unthinkingly happy. I was emerging from my bookish fantasy world and becoming more aware of the real one. In short, I was growing up.*

September Dreams

Labor Day dawned rainy and cold. Father was an agent for the Palo Farmers' Mutual Fire Insurance Company, and he felt fairly sure of finding most of his policyholders home on a day like this. He decided to make the rounds after he had taken Ray and three other ninth graders to Cook, thirty miles away. There they would "batch it" to stretch the stipend of six dollars a month the county allotted students too far from a high school to live at home.

Father set up his shaving mirror in the glassed-in porch, where the light was good, and hung his razor strop from a hook on the wall. With a soft shaving brush he worked up a thick white lather in the dish of shaving soap that smelled like Uncle Arvid's shop, lifted his chin and stretched his left cheek smooth so he could get every whisker. But the razor wasn't sharp enough to suit him. He wiped off the lather, pulled the leather strop taut, and deftly smacked the straight edge against it, first one side and then the other, with rhythmic slaps.

Vic came out of the kitchen, happy that summer was over and school was about to begin. "Father, before you go, could I have some money for new school shoes and a couple of shirts?"

Father pulled a hair from my head and severed it neatly with the razor to test its sharpness. He didn't look at Vic. He pulled the skin of his cheek taut once more and made a clean path across it. As he wiped the blade, he said, "You aren't going to school any more. I need you to help with all the farm work and lumbering."

Vic's mouth fell open. He ran a hand through his thick blond pompadour and blinked his light blue eyes behind his metal-rimmed glasses.

"Don't tease me, Father. You'd have told me before, not this last day before school. You wouldn't do that to me."

Father stropped his razor deliberately, humming a bit, hiding behind his jawful of lather, eyes fixed on his work. I escaped to the bedroom, picked Bobby up, and cuddled him so tightly that he looked at me in surprise before he decided not to cry. I sat down on the bottom step of the stairs, where I could look out to the porch through the sheer curtains of the kitchen window. I could hear the arguing voices, sometimes low and reasonable, sometimes hot and angry and saying ugly Finnish swear words. At first Father spoke as calmly and evenly as if he were convincing a meeting of the phone company that they needed to invest in new poles or to hire a man to cut the branches away from the wires.

"Listen, *poika*, I wouldn't tease you about something as serious as getting bread in our mouths and clothes on our backs. I thought you understood that being the oldest, and with a new mouth to feed, you have to be my helper now. But maybe you think you're so grown up that you can make all your own decisions. Let me tell you, I've taught you to be a good worker, and I need you to help. I'm not going to pay a hired man when I have a strong young son."

Now Vic's eyes filled with tears and his face turned red. He clenched his fists. He said thickly, "I don't believe you. You like to joke. You know I'll never be anything but a shit-shoveler if I can't finish high school."

Father stretched his cheek again, but didn't apply the razor. He peered into the mirror, glanced briefly at his son's dismayed face, and laid his razor on the wash stand.

"Enough! You should know I don't joke about things like this. You're not going to school and that's the end of it."

Vic shouted, "You *are* a tyrant after all. You're worse than *Poperikoffi*. You always said America's the land of opportunity, and so I thought I could even be an engineer. Now you want me to freeze in the woods and sleep with lice in a lumber camp all winter, or dig iron ore with a mile of dirt over my head, or pick rocks and shovel cow shit all my life! Maybe you think that kind of work would make me forget my ideas. But that's exactly the kind of slavery that makes people radical." He glared at Father and choked out, "Damn it to hell! I *am* going to school tomorrow."

Father's speech was much sharper than usual when he was angry; the Finnish "rr"s rattled harshly between the shortened vowels. "Shut your mouth, the devil take it to hell! You seem to think I'm *Herra* Hiltunen and you're some lord's son who doesn't have to dirty his hands. *Meikäläiset* can't be engineers. We have to work just to eat and keep clothes on our backs. Not another word!"

He wiped his face with a clean towel and examined his jaw. "Tomorrow we have to start fall plowing, and this winter we will lumber the homestead land. You're my helper now. That's how it has to be."

Face red, hands still clenched into tight fists, Vic stared at Father in disbelief. I scurried to the rocking chair just before he ran through the kitchen and up the stairs, flung himself down on his bed, and gave in to racking sobs that tore at his chest and scraped his throat. He tried to muffle them in the pillow, but I heard them as I rocked the baby, and my throat felt tight and choked up too.

Mother bustled in from milking, Mabel close at her heels lugging half a pailful of water with both hands. Mother started to talk about the day's errands, but fell silent at the sight of Father's grim clean-shaven face. She set down the milk pails in the porch, covered them with clean cloths, and rattled the grate of the kitchen stove to drown out the sounds from upstairs.

She went out to the porch. She asked Father, "What happened? Why is *Vikki* crying?"

"It's not your business," Father answered. "He's just being a child when he should be acting like a man. He'll get over his fancy ideas. Don't baby him."

Mother was still bewildered. "But *hyvänen aika*, what are you saying?"

"Only that he's going to be my work partner, not go to school to learn a lot of *turhaa*, useless stuff." His tone said that was the end of the matter. "Get me a clean shirt; I have to earn some money today."

Tight-lipped, Mother hung a clean white shirt on the edge of the mirror. She began to fill boxes with food for Ray to take along. As she worked, she shook her head as if she were trying to clear her mind of unbearable thoughts.

Ray came downstairs with a box of clothes and went out to pack his things in the car. I followed him and said, "How come you don't say a word about Vic? *You're* going to school. Why can't *he?*"

Ray's thin handsome face was unsmiling. "Keep your nose out of this. If I say anything I might get trapped too. But Father wants me to be another Paavo Nurmi and shine in all sports, so I'm not worried."

Father snatched his hat from the deer antlers by the stove, stalked out, and got into the driver's seat. When Ray climbed in, he drove off in a spray of muddy water. I had been with him on these insurance trips, and I pictured him strolling jauntily into a farm kitchen, laughing, joking, asking for coffee—his "away-from-home" personality.

After a while Mother went upstairs, and I crept up on the stairs to listen. I heard the bed creak as she sat down, and I could imagine her patting his shoulder. "Victor, I am so sorry. I had no idea. I should have guessed when Father asked Arvid to lend him money for a new car and Arvid said he had no business paying hired men when he had growing boys."

I heard him blow his nose. "Yeah, Arvid thinks barber college is enough education for anybody. I need to go to school more than Father needs a new car. He feels like a king behind the steering wheel, as if he's really made it in America."

"Listen, Victor," Mother pleaded. "He's so stubborn, I know it's no use for me to try to change his mind. Just try to get along with him, and next year I feel pretty sure you can go back to school. They're opening ninth and tenth grades in Embarrass, and you and Ray can go by bus, and you can both help him after school and weekends and vacations. And this winter you'll earn enough money so you won't have to ask him to buy you school clothes."

"That'll be the day. He didn't say a word about wages. He'll just dole out a dollar now and then as if I'm a little kid. Besides, if I get through tenth grade in Embarrass, I'll just be stuck again."

Bobby cried to be fed, and Mother came downstairs. I heard Vic snore; now and then a snore became a sob. After dinner he came downstairs, made himself a thick sandwich and drank some milk, and then, shoulders hunched against the rain, plodded across the field toward Matt's camp.

First day of school wouldn't be much fun this year, I thought, with everyone so sad and angry. Were we really so poor that we couldn't afford to let Vic work his way through high school? We'd had Otto Niemi or Uncle Ray or some other hired man every winter up to now.

I was so drowned in pity for Vic that it didn't occur to me that Father hated to take Vic out of school, and had put off telling him until there was no other choice. He knew no other way to tell him than the old authoritarian manner of the Finnish patriarch.

When Father came home for supper he said not a word, and I knew he would punish Mother by not speaking to her for a day or two. That much I knew. Now I realize that perhaps he was also punishing himself for his own ambivalent feelings of righteousness and guilt, and that perhaps Vic was right—he may have hoped, by working with Vic so closely, to persuade him to reconsider his radical tendencies.

Early next day, his eyes still red and swollen, Vic silently followed Father outside and harnessed the horses.

First day of school, a new teacher, a modern bus—and I would be in the upper grade room! Excitement built up, pushing concern for Vic out of my mind.

Mabel and I wore our crisp new dresses; Leo had a new plaid shirt and corduroy pants, with a jaunty cap Aunt Hulda had brought him. No longer did we have to ride in Mr. Hujanen's wagon-sleigh contraption. Neil Jokinen, who had married one of the Anderson girls at the end of the road, had a brand new station wagon, and when we saw him driving along the ridge above the potato field, we ran to reach the far gate just as he stopped for us.

The small nagging lump that had lodged in my throat since yesterday morning dissolved as I proudly entered the upper grade room with Leo. We were very curious about our new teacher, and sat prim and straight in our seats as we waited for her to begin the day. We knew her name from the list of teaching assignments in the *Duluth Herald*—Mabel Sivula. So at least she was Finnish. We were glad, because sometimes a *toiskielinen* or "other-tongued" teacher made us feel stupid and inferior, and chided those who spoke with a Finnish brogue.

Blonde and blue-eyed, with a high voice and a serious manner, which made her occasional wide, bright smile pleasing, Miss Sivula rapidly took us through her plans for the daily routine and her rules of deportment. Clearly, there was to be no "monkeying around" in her room, but she didn't seem as cranky and nervous as last year's upper grade teacher.

Best of all, she played the piano, and half an hour before dismissal time, she asked one of the boys to pass out the little tan song books, and she played "Flow Gently, Sweet Afton," "Swanee River," and "Old Zip Coon." I wished I could sing like Sivia Salmela and Elsie Dahl. I had learned the words to many of the old songs, and often sang them when I rocked the baby or roamed the woods, when it didn't matter that I couldn't carry a tune. Like some library books, these songs made me feel sentimental and romantic, or lively and merry, and helped me imagine places far beyond the little part of Minnesota that I knew.

Father sang beautifully, and I loved to hear him, but his songs were Old Country, and usually melancholy. Mother sang a lot too, usually because she was sad. She couldn't carry a tune any better than I, but singing cheered her up. Fetching firewood after school, I heard her singing "What a Friend We Have in Jesus" while she milked the cows. I knew she was thinking of Victor and wishing he were in school.

But at nine I was too self-centered, too much the eager schoolgirl, to mope long about the problems of others, even Vic and Mother. Though fifth graders were the "little kids" of the upper room, we felt very important when we were sent to fetch something from the stockroom. That treasure house was neatly piled with every conceivable color of construction paper, reams of white paper, lined and unlined, notebooks, ink, pens, pencils, crayons, watercolors, erasers, chalk, paper clips, and huge jars of paste. When we were sent to fill small jars from a large jar of paste, we dipped our fingers in the white stuff and giggled and said "Ish!" though we really liked to taste its super sweetness and perfect smoothness.

Only Teacher herself dissolved hectograph powder in boiling water and poured it into shallow trays, but when it was cold and set she often gave the master copy of a test to a couple of pupils from a grade other than the one taking the test. We pressed it carefully on the amber gel, wrinkled our noses at its acrid smell and tried not to smear the purple ink. Then we pressed sheets of shiny special paper on the gel and peeled each one off slowly so it wouldn't smear, until we had enough copies for the class. We were extra careful, too, if we were asked to cut paper with the heavy, wicked guillotine.

For some classes we were given used textbooks. Some were defaced with scribbled dirty words and drawings in defiance of the rule that you could write nothing but your name in the book, on the flyleaf. But for many subjects each of us was given a bright book that crackled with newness. Best of all, I thought, was each September's new array of beautiful library books.

Miss Sivula told us very seriously how lucky we were to live in St. Louis County, where tax money from the iron mines paid for public schools. "In some states, and even some Minnesota counties, you have to pay for your paper and pencils, and you hardly ever see new books," she said proudly.

When I repeated that to Victor one evening, he snorted. "Okay, that may be true, but they still don't pay miners decent wages, while they name Iron Range towns after themselves and build mansions in the big cities. You see any of *them* living in Tower, Buhl, Chisholm, and sending their kids to public school?"

Well, I shrugged, that was Vic's worry; to me, here and now, school was wonderful. Each month's report card gave me a feeling of accomplishment. I usually was proud to take mine home with grades in the 90s or even an occasional 100 (75 was passing) in Reading, Language, Arithmetic, Geography, History, Spelling, Grammar, Penmanship, Health, Civics, Drawing, Music, Agriculture, Physical Education, and Conduct. That last was sometimes my downfall; I was a talker and a clown, and disrupted more than one lesson with my antics.

Sometimes Mother signed the report cards, working her lips as she always did when she concentrated, and wrote in her firm clear hand, "Mrs. Peter Hiltunen." When Father took his turn I liked to watch him carefully produce his beautiful signature.

ୡୠୡୠୡୠୡୠୡୠ

Only 70 miles south of Canada, summers are short. If a Saturday in early September was sunny, it was potato picking day. If not, everyone took a day off from school, for many hands were needed to dig and pile up the potatoes and transport them to the root cellar, and fill baskets and gunnysacks to be sold in Tower and Virginia.

Before long, Mother was singing her autumn song. Mabel and I brought in colored leaves to be admired and pressed in heavy books between sheets of waxed paper. While we ate our after-school snack of fresh-baked bread with butter and jam or oatmeal cookies, Mother rocked Bobby and sang,

> Come, little leaves, said the Wind one day,
> Come over the meadows with me and play,
> Put on your dresses of red and gold,
> Summer has gone and the days grow cold . . .

In our free time Mabel and I "hunted quails" in the woods, throwing rocks or using slingshots when we spotted ruffed grouse in the underbrush. But unlike Father and the boys with their guns, we never brought game birds for a delicious dinner. We watched red squirrels run back and forth, cheeks full of winter provender to store in their nests in the hollows of trees. We ate brilliant red wintergreen berries that grew low among the pine needles, and filled our pockets with burry hazelnuts for the boys to husk. Sometimes we jumped and yelled for joy. The reds and yellows and oranges of maple and birch and poplar burned against dark green pines and bright blue sky, and affected us like a saturnalia before the penance of a long lenten winter. We plucked goldenrod, purple asters, Queen Anne's Lace, and pearly everlasting to take home. With Mother, we declaimed, changing the month to fit the Northland,

> O suns and skies and clouds of June,
> And flowers of June together,
> You cannot rival for one hour
> September's bright blue weather.

But the days were growing shorter and colder. When we came home from school one day, there sat two huge boxes from Sears Roebuck and Montgomery Ward. "I knew you'd want to open them," Mother said, "but don't think for a minute you got everything you put on those long lists from the wishing books."

We had lain on our stomachs on the rag rugs in our room for many hours, turned the pages of the thick Fall and Winter catalogs, and said, "I wanna get this dress . . . and that doll . . . and . . . and . . ."

Reality was opening the boxes and pulling out brown laced-up oxfords, ordinary buckled arctics, and simple wool melton coats—but at least these were a cheerful red.

But there were other things—a bright red sweater and a

gray skirt for me, and a light blue sweater and plaid skirt for Mabel, fluffy white angora tams for early winter, with scarves to match.

There were petticoats and warm bloomers and new garter vests, long underwear (Ish!) and lengths of soft flannel for new nightgowns. Diapers and warm clothes for Bobby. A new corset and a size 42 dress for Mother. A few new towels and several lengths of printed cotton to cover the wool batts that came from a mill in Bemidji where Mother sent old woolen clothes to be transformed into warm quilts. Flannel sheets to replace summer muslin. Uninteresting clothes for the menfolk, too.

The piles of warm clothing reminded us that winter was coming. So did the sight of Mother, seated in the rocking chair, knitting yet another pair of long black wool stockings with gray feet for Mabel and me, and mittens with braided cords to slip through the sleeves and over the shoulders to keep us from losing them. So, also, did the storm windows Father and Vic had put up that day, and the sound of axes ringing in the woods where they were felling trees for firewood. Indian summer could not last forever, any more than summer could.

The Tower High School.

First Snow

A chill rain fell from low gray clouds and turned to snow soon after we got to school one day in late October. As the snow whirled thicker and faster, its cold reflected light bathed the schoolroom in an eerie underwater glow. Like marine creatures, the children moved dreamily, one after another, to the pencil sharpener by the window, and as we watched the snow fall, our hands moved more and more slowly.

Teacher, too, gazed silently at the snow for minutes at a time. Then she shook her head as if to wake herself up, and spoke sharply, "Get back to work, all of you. We still have a lot to do today, and you'll be good and sick of winter before it's over—remember?"

But last winter was ages ago. Today the new snow promised wonderful things. Snowball fights, sliding, skiing, making snow angels and forts and snowmen and igloos. Dazzling white landscapes. Christmas!

After school, Mabel and I wanted to find big cardboard cartons on which to slide down the hill by the root cellar. But Mother had more practical plans.

"What if this snowfall turns into a blizzard and the root

The pines during a snowfall.

cellar door is blocked? The men haven't covered it with hay yet and it could freeze shut. We have to get plenty of food into the house right now."

We lit a lantern and climbed the slope a few yards to the slanting doors of the root cellar. Our breath made clouds in the air while we cleared away slippery wet leaves from the concrete steps.

"Open sesame!" I declaimed as we swung back the doors. In the dimness, we looked around at the stored abundance of summer. I went on with my fantasy as we filled a bushel basket with glass jars. "Ah, what treasures! Here are rubies, emeralds, and amethysts for the taking." Mother's mundane jars of beets, raspberries, blueberries, green beans and peas did indeed glimmer mysteriously like jewels in the lantern light. Even the yellow wax beans were gold. Who knew what those jams and jellies might really be? What did frankincense and myrrh look like?

When we brought the first load to the kitchen, Mother opened the trap door in the middle of the floor and climbed down the steep ladder to put the food away. Mabel shined a flashlight into the dark hole so Mother could see where to place the jars on the makeshift shelves of rough planks. A smell of damp moldy earth and Northern Spy apples came up from the cellar. As we

worked, we added the odors of potatoes, carrots, cabbages, rutabagas, and onions which we had dug from the damp sand in the
root cellar.

When Mother climbed out and let down the trap door,
pressing it firmly in place with both feet, she turned my fantasy
into solid, comforting reality. "Maybe we're not rich," she said,
"but we have lots to eat and warm clothes to wear, thank the Lord.
And we hardly made a dent in the root cellar today. Now the men
can cover it with hay so the rest of the food won't freeze, and the
door will be easier to open when we need more. Now, I'll go milk
the cows while you get supper on the table."

Father and Vic came in from their work in the woods,
stamped their boots in the porch, and tried to shake or brush the
snow from their coats and caps. Before Father could hang his
sheepskin coat on the deer antlers near the stove, Mabel ran and
hid under it. Father remembered their old winter game. "Where's
my *pikku piika*? I can't find her."

She giggled as he felt around with worried mutterings, then
exclaimed in surprise, "What's this? Miksi must have got in the
house. But this animal's saying 'tee-hee,' not *'rauf! rauf!' Hyvänen
aika!* It's *Meiboli!*"

She claimed her prize—a pink peppermint lozenge from the
ever-present little paper bag in his pocket.

Vic carefully lit the Aladdin lamp. He lifted it to see if there
was enough white gasoline in it for the evening, filled it to just
the right level, then pumped up the pressure with a silvery cylinder. He turned the little knob at the side to release gas into the
white silk mantles and held a long kitchen match close to each of
them, taking great care not to poke a hole in the delicate fabric.
When it caught fire, he adjusted the knob to the exact point where
no yellow flame flared to blacken the mantle. Two sharp blue
flames made the mantles glow with a brilliant white light that
flooded the room.

Father rubbed his back on the door jamb, but that wasn't
enough to relieve the strain and ache of the day's labor. He lay
face down on the long bedroom rug and asked Mabel to walk up
and down his back on her knees. He grunted just for fun as if she
were really hurting him. Then he groaned, *"Voi, Meiboli,* you're
better than that old *hieroja* that *Aiti* and I go to in Angora."

He and Vic took turns at the wash basin. They scooped
warm water out of the stove reservoir and scrubbed with gritty
Lava soap. Then they settled down to read the papers.

"Sure looks as if that *Hooveri* will be elected," Father said as I brought him the baby to rock until Mother came in from milking to nurse him. "And I'm pretty sure Jacob Pete will be Road Commissioner for northern St. Louis County and I'll get a good job."

The local Finns were much more excited about this post than about the presidency. Politicians sought out Father because of his gift of gab and leadership. He supported Jacob Pete, the Finnish candidate, against William Faye, the *toiskielinen* incumbent. One day he saw a Finnish supporter of Faye in the Tower shoemaker shop and remarked sarcastically to the other customers as well as his own companions, "Here's our fine *Suomalaisuuden esikuva!*" (example of Finnish unity). The words were widely quoted. So were those of a letter Mother wrote to the *Päivälehti*, calling the man a traitor to his people. Mother was pleased when people laughed and quoted her strong phrases, which were highly uncharacteristic of a Finnish farmer's wife.

Vic cared much more about the national election. He rattled the front page of the *Duluth Herald* and said, "Yup, those big capitalists will win again. Maybe Al Smith would do something for the workers, but the voters won't go for a Catholic. The bullshit Hoover hands out will get the votes. Here he goes again with that stuff about the vanishing poorhouse, two chickens in every pot and a car in every garage."

When Mother came in he turned to the funnies.

Victor was a politically precocious fifteen-year-old, but at nine I was still much more interested in Halloween and Christmas. All through October, grinning jack-o-lanterns and black witches on broomsticks decked the windows and walls at school. During the last hour on Halloween day, we bobbed for apples in galvanized washtubs and, hands behind our backs, tried to eat the sugar-powdered doughnuts that dangled tantalizingly from string tied across a corner of the room. We played Farmer in the Dell, Blindman's Buff, and Musical Chairs. The teachers gave us each a cup of apple cider, a rare treat so far north of apple country.

That evening the boys went out for a little mischief. They rattled notched thread spools on window panes, emitted eerie wolf-like howls, and tipped over the none-too-solidly anchored toilet of a none-too-popular person. Next day they looked innocent, but exchanged knowing glances while we replaced the October decor with Pilgrims, Indians, and turkeys.

Hoover and Jacob Pete were both elected. And Tiistikki (Tuesday's Child) had a heifer calf, which Mother named Electa for Election Day. (Later, on Inauguration Day, another calf was born and went through life as Hooveretta.) The new calf was more important to Mother than the election. For me, the greatest victory of the day was the curds and whey Mother made from the new milk and sprinkled with sugar and cinnamon.

Of immediate interest to the menfolk was the coming of hunting season. Legal hunting season, that is. Already a skinned carcass hung frozen in the shed. Mother would send Father or one of the big boys to slice off enough for a roast or stew. She liked the frozen meat because the fat came off easily, and there was no gamy taste. The smaller children simply took it all for granted, enjoying the meat as well as the stories about spotting and shooting deer and outwitting game wardens.

Father was locally famous for his prowess with a deer rifle. He had taught the boys to watch for deer in early morning or just before sundown at a salt lick in the spring, headlight them on summer nights, track them in the snow, always aim for a buck—never a doe or fawn—and to shoot clean.

On the way home from an evening out visiting, Father often shined a spotlight from the car around the sides of the road and into the woods. If he spotted a deer, he would hurry home to clamp on a carbide lamp. The powerful optic lens of its headlight was an effective—though illegal—means of locating and blinding deer.

But the deer now hanging in the shed was his "dream deer." He woke one Sunday morning from a dream that there were two deer on the hill behind the house. He pulled on his clothes and grabbed his rifle. He didn't even bother to put in his false teeth. He found the deer's tracks in the fresh snow and shot the buck.

Again we were cleaning frantically, for not only were Uncle Arvid and Aunt Hulda coming, but also their friends, the Pehkonens. Again Mabel and I had to sleep on the bedroom sofa. Again we had to act grateful for used clothes, most of which, Mother whispered, would make nice carpet rags. But we were glad to see them nonetheless and were happy with our new woolen hats, scarves, and mittens, and a bag of candy apiece. We sat on the stairs and munched our candy while we listened to our relatives regale the visitors with deer-hunting stories.

There was an inexhaustible supply of stories, too, from way back when Vic guided a warden to a barrel of cow piss near the vegetable garden (Mother believed it made good fertilizer), to the time Uncle Felix found Father playing cribbage with the game warden himself while a venison stew simmered on the stove.

❁❁❁❁❁❁❁❁❁❁

Father was also known as an amateur blood letter. Uncle Arvid had told Mr. Pehkonen of his skill with the little *suonirauta*, or "vein iron." The ruddy-faced, stout visitor asked Father if losing some blood might ease his high blood pressure. They went out to the end of the house together, and Mr. Pehkonen bared his arm. Father swiped the knife across the seat of his pants and held the arm steady with his left hand as he quickly made a deft cut in the vein at the elbow. (I was watching, fascinated and horrified, from the bedroom window while the others went on talking around the coffee table.)

The men watched thick blood spurt out on the snow. Father pressed on the cut, folded a clean cloth in the elbow, telling him to hold it there for a few minutes. As sure of himself as a doctor, he said, "Yes, you were right. You had too much blood and it's too thick."

By the end of the week, Uncle Arvid and Mr. Pehkonen each had a deer. We never inquired too closely as to who had fired the fatal shots—the city visitors or their country cousins. Whoever it was, Uncle Arvid and Mr. Pehkonen each posed proudly while Aunt Hulda clicked the Brownie. Red cap rakishly tilted, rifle held nonchalantly along one arm, each man planted one foot like a conquering hero on the flank of his trophy. Then they draped a deer over each of the front fenders of the Chevrolet, making sure the magnificent antlers were displayed for the camera (and for anyone they might pass on the road). Finally they drove off, beaming, warm with coffee and pancakes, back to the city.

Mabel and I turned thankfully back to our own room and to thoughts of Thanksgiving and Christmas.

A Finnish-American Christmas

We celebrated Thanksgiving in a thoroughly American fashion. Driving to Grandpa's house for dinner, we sang "Over the River and Through the Woods." Aunt Helen, Uncle Charlie, and cousins Albert, Arne and Irene were already there. Soon Aunt Lydia arrived from Ely with Uncle Herman and our cousins Walter and Delores. With Grandpa, Uncles Ray and Felix, and Aunt Hilma, our gang of eight Hiltunens brought the total to twenty-one, all crowded happily into Grandpa's small house.

Our menu didn't include a turkey this time, but our fat chickens were just as good. When the last bit of pumpkin pie slathered with whipped cream was gone, the men laid their stuffed bodies down for a nap. The cousins cleared the tables. Then the aunts and Mother shooed us away so they could gossip over the dishes.

The cousins had important business. It was our only chance to be together to plan the "program" for Christmas Eve. Though I tended to be bossy, in this I deferred to Cousin Walter, the acknowledged genius of the clan.

Each year we put on a pageant, sang carols, and recited a

poem or two. Each year—how this was a tradition when I was only nine I can't remember—we also put on a new play. Walter wrote and directed it in the short time we had left on Thanksgiving afternoon before Aunt Lydia and family drove home to Ely.

At age ten, Walter already looked like a haughty scholar. He had a hawk nose and a thin-lipped smile that turned down at the corners. His way of running his hand through his combed-back blond hair and closing his pale blue eyes when he was annoyed or impatient with his slower cousins—all this intimidated us. Planning the program, he sat crouched against the bedroom wall, elbows on knees and hands curled over his eyes, and demanded quiet. "I'm thinking!" he hissed.

In a few minutes he had an idea for a play. He cast the characters, gave us our lines, and warned us to learn them well by Christmas Eve.

Before we left, we wrote each relative's name on a slip of paper and made sure everyone drew a name out of a hat. That way each of us would have to buy only one Christmas gift, and everyone was sure to receive at least one. We did the same thing in school, but a lot of swapping and bargaining went on there. A child rebelled at giving a gift to someone he either hated or might be suspected of liking—if that person was of the opposite sex.

❈❈❈❈❈❈❈❈❈❈

The school Christmas program was the most exciting event of the whole year. After Thanksgiving, school work took a back seat to preparations and practice for that occasion.

The teachers chose a play for the upper grades and one for the lower grades, taught carols for all of us to sing together (and others for a few chosen singers), and chose some of us to recite poems and monologues. They rehearsed another group in a "drill" in which the costumed children moved through their paces on the stage, each carrying one letter of "Merry Christmas," and finally, as they stood in a row that spelled out the message, each pupil recited a brief verse appropriate to his or her letter. Then they all shouted, "Merry Christmas!"

This year, as always, there was a silent pageant showing the Holy Family and the shepherds and Wise Men, with Miss Sivula playing "Silent Night" softly. A seven-year-old whose front teeth were missing was coached to recite a short poem en-

Typical Christmas play costumes at School 40. Note the long underwear each girl wore.

titled "Chrithmeth," sure to bring a laugh from the audience and murmurs of "How cute!" from mothers.

While one teacher directed rehearsals, the other helped with decorations: chains of green and red loops of construction paper, yards of tinsel rope, glittery letters spelling out Christmas messages. There were huge posters of jolly Santas and flat shapes that unfolded into honeycombed red and white bells to hang from the ceiling.

Two or three fathers built a temporary stage at one end of the upper-grade room. The teachers had them nail up a rope that would hold the stage curtains fashioned of white sheets. The men put up a tall tree, and the teachers helped the older children decorate it. Finally, it was the last day of school before Christmas vacation. We all went home in great excitement to prepare for the wonderful evening.

It was bitterly cold that day. Aunt Pearl had sent us new dresses from Minneapolis; she worked at Munsingwear. Mine was a red wool jersey hanging in soft folds from a beige yoke. Mabel's was the same style in soft blue. Even though it was 50 below zero, we stubbornly refused to wear our black woolen stockings. Mother compromised by insisting on long underwear. I hated the process of holding the underwear legs around my ankles while

I tried to slide on my tan cotton stockings without leaving a tell-tale baggy place. Mabel and I helped each other struggle with the lumps. Then we took out the strips of rags from our hair that had produced curls and brushed out each other's hair—mine turning auburn rather than blonde by now. We checked each other to see that our petticoats didn't show.

Father had decided not to cope with the car. He would have had to fire the stove in the garage all day to keep the car warm enough to start, and go outside every ten minutes or so during the program to warm up the motor. Instead, the long sleigh on its heavy runners stood in front of the house. He and the boys piled it full of hay and covered that with thick horse blankets. Mother had heated bricks in the oven for hours to keep us warm during the two-mile ride.

Somehow we were all ready to leave by six-thirty. Bobby looked like a little mummy—only his nose and bright, wondering eyes peeked through the swaddling blankets. Victor helped Mother climb in with Bobby, and all but Father huddled down in the hay and lay back. Father said, "Giddyap, Billy. Giddyap, Yimmy," and the sleigh pulled away, its runners squeaking on the dry snow. Mabel and I snuggled together, marveling at the clear winter sky spangled with trillions of stars.

Eager though we were to get to school in plenty of time for the program, the ride seemed short. We left our parents and Vic to find seats in the upper room as we hurried into the lower room, hung our wraps in the cloakroom and kicked off our arctics. We all preened at the compliments our schoolmates freely dispensed. "Oh, Hilda, what a pretty dress!" "Emily, who curled your hair?" "Elsie, with a curling iron."

The teachers made sure each child knew where his or her costumes and drill cards were. They repeated the signals for marching in, and the order of the various pieces chalked on the blackboard, complete with names. They straightened this boy's tie, slicked down that one's stubborn cowlick, pinned up a petticoat.

"Now boys and girls," Miss Sivula said in her high nervous voice, "I know you will all do your best. If you make a mistake, just go right on; if you forget, look at me and I'll prompt you. I'm going in now to announce the program, and Miss Nikkinen will tell you when to come in for the first song."

Cheeks red from cold and excitement, tummies clutched to quiet their butterflies, we found it hard to keep quiet. Miss Nikkinen warned us that our parents couldn't hear the program if we were noisy. She reminded us to fetch our wraps from the cold cloakroom and put them on desks to warm up before the last carol.

When the piano struck the first notes of "Hark the Herald Angels Sing," we marched in, the tallest first so they could stand in the back row, the little ones last, in the front row. I was in the middle row, and sang lustily until Sivia, beside me, poked her elbow into my ribs. I knew the signal; I was flat, and would throw everyone else off key unless I simply moved my lips. Oh, well, I had an important part—I was the Mother in "The Birds' Christmas Carol."

During the drill, we heard sudden laughter, quickly muffled, and when the group returned, asked what had happened.

"Oh, that dumb Toivo stood in the wrong place, and it said, 'M-E-R-Y-R' until we made him move."

"Aw shut up, smarty! You know Teacher just changed my place today, and I forgot."

The pageant and plays went smoothly, the applause for every poem and monologue was satisfying, and finally it was time for the closing number, "Silent Night." Afterwards, the children remained on stage. A loud "Ho, ho, ho!" from the hall signaled the entrance of Santa Claus, in American-style red and white.

The little ones were wide-eyed. The big kids nudged one another and whispered that it was really Helmer Koski, who had the biggest belly around. He passed out string bags of hard candy and sticky pink popcorn balls tied in red net, then distributed the teachers' gifts to the children, and ours to those whose names we'd drawn. Two or three parents had brought gifts for their children, and Mother's lips pursed in disapproval. She had told us this was a way of showing off and made the poorer kids feel bad.

For a few minutes the room was noisy and busy with children asking their parents, "Did you see me? Did you think I was good?" Before long, everyone was dressed for the cold once more, and we left, calling "Merry Christmas" wishes to everyone in sight.

All the way home we sang, our voices thin and clear in the crisp air—flat or in tune, it no longer mattered. It was fun to shout "Jingle Bells" in rhythm with the horses' trotting and the jingling of their harness.

Already the house was cold. Father and Vic stoked the

fires and lit the bright Aladdin lamp. Mother warmed up coffee for the grownups and made cocoa for the kids.

"Was I good?" I asked for the fifth time.

Seated around the table, we opened the presents from our teachers—a comb for Leo and handkerchiefs for Mabel and me. We investigated the candies, all red, green, and white; some had roses in the center and a red coating around the outside of a white cylinder. Some were ripples of red and white or green and white stripes. Best of all, Reino had drawn my name and ignored possible teasing; I was thrilled with a box of stationery, every sheet and envelope adorned with a pink rose.

⍺⍺⍺⍺⍺⍺⍺

When we calmed down a little, Mother sent us to bed. "This was only the first program," she reminded us. "There's one here Christmas Eve and one at church the Sunday after Christmas, so get a lot of rest."

I paused on the stairs and said, "Oh, Father, I'm so glad we went in the sleigh. It was much more fun than the car, and besides, last year you didn't hear my poem because you were outside warming up the car."

Though the cocoa had warmed our tummies, our feet were still cold. We took turns putting them between each other's thighs to warm them while we talked about the dolls we hoped to get from—well, Santa Claus, of course. Mother thought we still believed in him, and we didn't want to risk telling her otherwise. It was never harder to get to sleep than when we were full of Christmas cheer. Mother had to call "Gur-rulls!" several times before our whispers and giggles ceased.

⍺⍺⍺⍺⍺⍺⍺

Mother had already started her Christmas baking. She had made Cousin Jack fruitcake and put it away to ripen. She called it a poor man's version because it used fewer nuts and candied fruits and more raisins than fancier recipes.

Mabel and I loved helping her cut out and decorate molasses cookies in the shape of Santas, bells, Christmas trees, snowmen, and deer, and spread powdered-sugar icing on braided wreaths of egg bread redolent of cardamom—our usual biscuit decorated for Christmas with candied cherries and bits of green crystallized citron. We had to be especially careful with Finnish prune tarts. We shaped squares of Mother's delicate pastry into pinwheels and carefully gathered their points together over a generous dab of prune jam.

Father and the boys chopped down the prettiest, most symmetrical balsam they could find, made a stand for it, and set it up by the far window of the other room, at the foot of the bed. The younger children rummaged in the boys' room pantry for boxes stored away a year ago, holding old-fashioned cardboard ornaments edged in gilt lace, tinsel ropes tarnished from years of use, balls of colored glass that had survived, and metal clips to hold candles on the branches. We added a box of glistening new balls that Mother had bought in Tower. We mixed flour and water to make paste, and joined strips of red and green construction paper to make chains, and draped them on the tree.

Then we carefully clipped at the ends of the branches the green, red and white candles we would light for brief periods—with a pail of water handy. We rather envied city folks their strings of colored electric lights, but they lacked the soft radiance of those candles. Finally, we draped the tree with heavy aluminum icicles that glimmered mysteriously even in the dim firelight of the wood-burning heater.

We had to wait until Christmas Eve to put our little piles of wrapped presents under the tree. One reason was that by now Bobby could crawl to investigate things in a flash. The other was that this year we were going shopping in Virginia. Oh, lovely phrase. To "go shopping" was to be like city people. For previous Christmases Mabel and I had had to make our gifts with paper, paste, and crayons, or scraps of cloth and embroidery floss. But 1928 was different.

We had hoarded money visitors had given us, and dimes from the summer road workers at the nearby gravel pit, to whom we had taken coffee and coffee bread Mother had prepared. Three days before Christmas Father took all the children—except, of course, Bobby—the twenty long miles to Virginia.

On this damp gray day the street lights shone with misty auras. Between each pair of lamp posts, their round white globes like clusters of huge grapes atop black iron standards, a string of colored lights stretched across the street and spelled out a Christmas greeting or wishes for a happy New Year. A lighted tree winked from every store window, and carols pealed from somewhere unseen.

Mabel and I stopped only briefly in front of the more elegant stores to admire their displays, then headed for the ones we could afford. We roved the aisles of Woolworth's, Kresge's, and McClellan's in an agony of indecision. The bright lights, the milling shoppers, the smells of candy and popcorn and damp wool, and most of all the hundreds of things appealing to be bought—all of these made our heads swim.

Finally we chose a flour sifter for Mother because she had complained about the old one during our Christmas baking, and a clump of red berries and holly leaves to pin on her coat. We knew she needed a new eggbeater and wanted a pretty cake plate, too; maybe by Mother's Day we would save enough again. Father always seemed to like a red bandanna handkerchief. It was easy to decide on an ash tray for Uncle Felix, whose name I had drawn. But Cousin Walter, with his biting wit? Mabel finally chose a paperweight for his study table simply because she liked the way the snow fell around the Swiss cottage when you turned it over; let him make what wisecracks he pleased.

But, oh how many toys for babies, and how small the handful of coins we still clutched inside our mittens! At last we decided that Bobby would be happy with a bright red ball with tinkling bells inside. Then we separated to buy each other's gifts, which on Christmas Eve turned out to be identical bottles of cologne. (That sounded glamorous. I don't think we would have bought anything called toilet water.)

When we left town, the gray day had turned miserably windy and sleety. Halfway home, the radiator boiled over. Vic got out in the stinging sleet and with his heavy gloves on, carefully unscrewed the hot radiator cap and let clouds of steam evaporate before he poured in water from the emergency can. He scraped frost from the windshield. Even the special frost shield taped in front of the driver was caked with sleet. Mabel whispered, "I'm glad this didn't happen on the way to town; we might never have gone."

At mail time that week, Mother always found more urgent tasks for Mabel and me than fetching the mail. After it came, she looked downcast for a long while, and was quiet and thoughtful. Even the mail of the 24th disappointed her. Vic braved the seven icy miles to Tower to fetch the afternoon mail. When he came home, she looked inquiringly at him. He shook his head and handed her a small package.

But Mabel and I hardly noticed, we were so excited about the gathering of the relatives, the dinner, the program. By late afternoon the house gleamed with cleanness and was decked with tinsel and paper chains and honeycomb bells. The boys milked the cows while Mother prepared a turkey. She was just changing into a clean dress and apron when three carloads of smiling relatives came in bearing gifts and food. No matter that their coats were piled high on the sewing machine in the corner behind the door and hung in layers on the pegs above it, their mittens and galoshes crowded around and atop the woodbox. The table was set for the clan, the tree exhaled its promise of delight, dinner was delicious, and at last it was time to take chairs into the other room and listen to our program. Vic and Ray carefully lit the candles on the tree, and their soft bright glow was the most magical part of Christmas.

Ray sat at the organ and played and sang "O Holy Night" to set a religious mood. The next two pieces, though they mentioned a favorite saint and an undefined Heaven, were more concerned with gifts and goodies.

I recited—with great drama, I thought—"A Visit from Saint Nicholas" while the others got into costume. Then I slipped an old torn housedress over my new red Christmas dress to play a little orphaned match girl gazing wistfully into the window of a fancy toy shop. A rich family, dressed in furs and silks and satins, took her home and showered her with wonderful food and mountains of toys. She woke up in death, frozen, and found she was in Heaven. When the grownups applauded long and hard, Walter said to me in a half-smiling aside, "Oh, I knew they would like something sweet and sentimental."

Then I read the Christmas story from Saint Luke for our pageant of the birth of Jesus. This year Mabel had a real baby to hold as she sat on a pillow, mantled in blue and surrounded by Leo as Joseph, and by our cousins draped in towels and carrying tree limbs to represent shepherds' crooks. Then Walter, Albert and Arne were transformed into the Three Wise Men, pacing in with their gifts while Ray played and sang, "We Three Kings of Orient Are." When they knelt, he shifted to "Silent Night," and sang the last verse so softly we all hushed, and even Bobby lay quiet, his eyes wide with wonder at the lights and music.

The program over, we were taking off crowns and fake beards and bath towel cloaks when we heard someone stamp his feet in the porch. A deep voice asked, in Finnish, "Are there any good boys and girls in this house? I have toys for them, but the bad ones will get only ashes and sticks."

A bearded figure in a sheepskin coat and hat entered, carrying a lumpy gunnysack flung over a shoulder. He was the *Joulupukki*, the Finnish Santa Claus. He gave out small presents—tops, balls, games of Old Maid—to the children and then shared out the presents under the tree, and vanished before all the confusion of unwrapping and exclaiming and thanking was over. No dolls. Well, Mabel and I told each other, they'll be in our stockings in the morning.

We woke up before dawn when we heard the door of the bedroom stove clang shut. We tiptoed downstairs. Our stockings hung limp over a chair by the tree, only a small bulge in the toe. "Go back to bed, girls," said Mother. "It's much too early."

Glancing back at the glimmering tree shining in the firelight, we did as we were told. When we woke again, it was bright day, and we hurried down for our dolls.

Mother tried to talk cheerfully. "I'm sorry, girls, Santa Claus must have made a mistake. I'm sure he got the wrong house and he'll bring the dolls later." We tried to look happy with our new coloring books and crayons, painted tin tea sets, and the dime and orange we always found in the toe of each stocking. If we had clung to a shred of faith in Santa, it was destroyed now.

But Mother looked so sad we knew we hadn't fooled her. We went upstairs with our meager toys and cried softly for a while. Then bright sunshine told us it was a perfect day to go sliding. We could have a tea party later, when the grownups had Christmas morning coffee.

The slope from the door of the root cellar down to the barnyard gate was soon slick from our repeated swoops down the hill on pieces of cardboard.

Leo was disappointed in Christmas too. He had loudly and repeatedly let Father and Mother know he wanted a shiny sled with steel runners. But he had to remain content with the makeshift one Otto had fashioned of wood a couple of winters before, when he helped Father with the work Vic had now taken over. Once in a while Leo gave us girls a ride on it.

Ray enjoyed winter more than anyone else in the family. He had piled snow into a ski jump on the longer slope, the one toward the road, and poured water on it so it would freeze firm and slick. Now, in his heavy dark red sweater, with its shawl collar around his neck and a knitted cap pulled over his ears, he swooped down the hill and took off again and again for an airborne jump, and landed victorious on the gentler slope of the yard.

Vic went off to visit Eino, shrugging off Mother's protest that he should share Christmas Day with his family. "I won't be gone long," he said.

I was shocked to hear him mutter as he banged the porch door shut, "Jesus Christ, I'm fifteen and they treat me like a kid."

When he showed up shortly before supper, Mother said, "I can tell from the smell you've been to Matt's camp."

"Merry Christmas, Maw," he grinned, and went to help Ray with the separator.

❊❊❊❊❊❊❊❊❊❊❊

Next day after mail time, Mother said she had to look at Electa, and gave Mabel the baby to rock and asked me to make sandwiches for dinner. Soon she was back, holding something behind her and beaming. "Imagine, girls, Santa Claus made a mistake," she said happily. "He left your presents in the barn hayloft."

She handed each of us a box. Inside were the dreamed-of dolls—exquisite young ladies with long stiff movable arms and legs and slim bodies, frilly white dresses and bonnets, one edged in blue and one in pink, curly auburn hair, and dark blue eyes that closed when you laid them down. We were enchanted.

"They're called Flossie Flirts," she told us, "but you can give them any name you want. Leo got a new sled that was hidden up there too."

After supper the Niemela family came to visit. We showed off our dolls and played tea party with the girls by the Christmas tree in the other room while the grownups sat at the coffee table. When I went into the kitchen to get milk for our teacups, I heard Mother say, "I sold so many subscriptions to *The Woman's World* and *The Farmer* and *The Farmer's Wife* that I earned two dolls for the girls, and I ordered a sled for Leo with cream money, and I was so mad because they didn't come in time for Christmas."

I tiptoed back to the girls and resumed my role of hostess. But my mind was elsewhere. At last I decided Mother was a good actress and Christmas had been wonderful after all. Then I stuck out my little finger and played lady again.

Snowbound

Leo was so happy with his new Flexible Flyer that he went out sliding even after supper. When he called out, "Car coming!" Mabel and I had already seen car lights stop at the far gate, and hurried to sweep the floor and straighten the rag rugs. The visitors were Father's *omanpaikkasia* from Embarrass, the Ahos, with two children.

When the boys were tired of sledding, they came upstairs to see the animal furs Leo claimed for his own and hoped to sell. Laila Aho had been telling us about their summer trip, and could not remember where Nashwauk was. She asked her brother, "Hey Ilmari, where's Nashwauk?"

"It iss where it hass pin pefore," he answered.

Mabel and I couldn't help it. We laughed so hard we rolled on the floor. Laila and Ilmari laughed too, taking our hilarity as a tribute to his wit.

When we woke up next morning, the wind had risen and snow was falling in gusts and swirls. I nearly choked with laughter as I repeated Ilmari's Finnish brogue. Vic took me to task. "Don't be too sure you talk that much better. Just wait till you go away from Peyla to a place where there are hardly any Finns. You might be laughed at too."

"But Vic," I protested, "you mock the Pike boys when they say 'Beyla poys blay pall,' instead of 'Peyla boys play ball.'"

"Okay, that's an old joke, but the kids in Pike and Embarrass have more of a brogue than we do in Vermilion or Peyla or whatever you want to call it because they don't have as many other nationalities there as we do, and hardly any of their parents speak English. You know this place was called Peyla for a long time because Italians named Peyla settled here and handled the mail for years. Anyway, other people make enough fun of Finns without us doing it too."

The snowfall became a blizzard, the kind that might go on for days. We all had special jobs for snowbound days. Father put Ray and Leo to carrying enough firewood to fill half the porch. Father and Vic fetched saws to sharpen, and went upstairs to sit by the boys' room window, where east light came in. As Mother was going out with her milk pails, she said, "After you wash dishes, girls, empty the top of the sideboard—and the drawers too. It looks like a ship about to sail."

"The cargo's sure not stowed away shipshape," Vic remarked on his way upstairs with a file.

"'Course not. Everybody just throws junk in the drawers or on top," I retorted. We transferred the jumble of papers and oddments on the sideboard to the kitchen table, wiped its top carefully, and polished it with dark Old English Wax. We emptied the two small top drawers and sat down to sift through the mess.

Father had served or was serving as township tax assessor, township supervisor, Farmer's Club president, member of the board of directors of the two-store Embarrass Co-operative Association, founder and president of the Pike River Telephone Company, and fire insurance agent, and we didn't dare do more with his papers than clean his drawer and return the papers as neatly as we could.

When Mother came in from milking, we had done the grubby part and reached the big drawer, where snapshots and studio pictures and old books were stored. Mother fetched the coffee grinder from the pantry, poured some beans into the top, and sat down to grind them. She emptied the delicious smelling coffee into the pot and put it on the stove to reach a boil. Bobby cried when he heard her voice. She fetched him and put him in the high chair, then cracked an egg and dropped the shell into the coffeepot to clear the grounds before she sat down to nurse him. This was a good time to ask her questions.

Mabel held up our favorite picture. "Oh, that one," Mother laughed, "was taken almost 12 years ago, when Uncle Arvid caught up with us one morning before I had time to fix up."

Mother, in a dust cap and long dress and apron, stood stoutly behind three little tow-headed boys. Father wore a cap and baggy-kneed overalls; he looked very slim and young. Beside them was an open four-wheel buggy. In its shafts stood a sway-backed horse. The house was still very clearly a log cabin; the big glassed-in porch and white-painted siding hadn't been added. But what made the picture look most like ancient history was the one scraggly pine on the hill behind the house. We remembered only tall Norway and white pines.

I lingered over an old Finnish Bible, its cover long since gone. I marveled at the Gothic print, with "s"s shaped like "f"s, in an old copy of the *Kalevala* that Father's mother had sent him before she died. That was her picture, the sad sepia one with a curl of brown hair inside the glass.

"What's a *Kalevala*?" I asked.

Mother stacked up the rest of the books and pictures and put them back in the drawer. The men would be wanting their mid-morning coffee. She got out cups and saucers, and as she set the table, she told me, "The *Kalevala*. It's the old Finnish epic poem. It's beautiful, but it's too hard for you to understand yet."

Father was already at the table waiting for coffee. He recited a few lines, slowly and rhythmically. . . something like *"Kantoi kuuta kaksi, kolme,"* and *"vaka vanha Väinämöinen."*

"But that sounds just like 'Hiawatha'!" I said.

Vic assured us that was no accident. "Longfellow got the idea for that meter from the *Kalevala*. And you know that little lap harp Walter Maniko plays? It's the Finnish *kantele*, mentioned in the *Kalevala*—an ancient magic instrument."

Vic stoked the stoves and went back upstairs. I gazed at the swirling snow, covering the road and putting caps on the fence posts. I heard Mother rummaging in the boys' room pantry and knew she was finding another job for us.

Mother came downstairs carrying a bulging cardboard carton and Vic followed her with another. "Carpet rag time, girls," she said, "the perfect entertainment for weather like this."

She found us each a pair of scissors and showed us just how

wide to cut the strips of cloth from the old clothes in the boxes, going round and round so the strips would be as long as possible. Mabel sneezed.

Mother sympathized. "I know it's a boring chore, but they're all clean. That's lint, not dust. And as soon as I put Bobby to bed and put potatoes and a roast in the oven, I'll cut some too and tell you about pioneer days."

Rag rugs up to a yard wide and of many different lengths covered the floors of every Finnish house. As muddy feet and frequent washing took their toll, older ones were laid over porch and sauna dressing room benches, and even on the toilet floor. Spread in summer shade, they offered inviting places for naps and reading and visits.

We needed new ones, and had to get the strips cut and rolled into balls for old Mrs. Simonson. She had brought her big heavy wooden loom from Finland and spent long hours weaving rugs for a small cash income.

From her loom these strips would emerge as dark, heavy rugs, the shreds of winter pants, shirts, and coats; as deep red ones from old flannel sheets Mother had dyed in the copper boiler in the sauna; as tweedy blue ones that once had been men's summer overalls and shirts; and as bright ones of rainbow stripes—the ghosts of summer dresses.

Mother picked up her scissors and sat down. She chose a thick plaid flannel shirt, out at the elbows, that all three older boys had worn in turn, cut off the buttons and carefully started cutting a strip. Finally, she began to talk.

"The olden days. They don't feel like ancient history to me —not like the Greeks and Romans you study in school. But I guess they do to you."

She pondered a moment. Her mouth worked in rhythm with the snipping and crunching of her scissors. "Let's see. I think I'll tell you about 'Athens, Paradise.' "

Our scissors stopped clicking, and we looked up. This was a new story. Mother looked at us sharply. "But I won't tell it unless you can listen and work at the same time. School starts again Monday, and I want all these done."

We quickly bent our heads and began snipping.

"Well, you know Mama and Pa came up the Old Vermilion Trail in a horse-drawn wagon when I was just a baby, because Virginia was a boom town in the 1890s. Pa got a job in the mine, and Mama ran a boarding house and kept cows—I told you about that, and how hard she worked. Then Pa got a kind of pneumonia. The doctor called it 'mine fever' and told him to quit the job and live where the air was pure. So Pa thought of taking our cows out to the country and homesteading a piece of land."

She stopped to listen as the rasp of a file on a saw tooth turned to a screech. "I was afraid Bobby was awake already," she said.

"Well, Mama thought that was fine, just so it was near good water—a river or a lake. She was glad to get away from the rough saloons and the brawling miners and lumberjacks, and the muddy streets, even though she would miss the Temperance Society and the coffee socials and church meetings. And there had been two terrible fires that burned many houses—and we lived in a wooden house near a lumber yard.

"Pa did find a lovely spot near a lake, where he still lives, and he staked a claim to 160 acres of it under the Homestead Act. He moved out there with two friends from Kauhajoki to get it ready for the family. First they built a rustic cabin and then, across the swamp from it, a two-room log cabin." We had stopped cutting to imagine Grandpa's lake in those days, but she had that faraway look and didn't notice.

"We moved on December 4, 1904, when I was going on eleven. I remember how early we had to get up in the dark to go to the depot. I think Mr. Matala, who had a horse and sleigh, took us there. About noon, I guess, we got to our stopping place. It was just a platform along the Duluth and Iron Range Railroad—a place called Athens. Snow was falling gently. It was a beautiful day."

She was gazing out at the snowfall. Suddenly she snapped out of her trance and said, "I guess I stopped cutting too. Let's get busy now." We all bent our heads over our work and snipped very hard for a few minutes. Then she went on.

"A couple of days earlier my Uncle Christian, Pa's brother, and Aunt Alina had taken three of our cows, tied somehow to a mule-drawn sleigh, the thirty miles in the winter weather. Uncle Christian met us at Athens with the mule team.

"When we got to the cabin, Mother wanted to see how the cows had fared. She gave me Felix to hold; he was a year old. I went indoors and sat down on a lower bunk holding him and wondering, everything being so new and different, and *all* of a *sudden* I heard a shot, and a bullet whizzed *right* behind my head."

Mother was stressing some words even more than she usually did, and the whine of the saws being sharpened upstairs added an eerie note to her story.

"The baby screamed and I screamed. If I had moved my head backwards an *inch* we would both have been killed. Richard was six, and he had found a loaded gun under one of the bunk beds and fired it right toward us. Well! They knew outside that something had happened, and Mama just about fainted, and Pa came in and I said, 'I'm all right. *Riku* took the gun.' They could see the bullet hole in the wall. He had to find out everything and test everything. I think it was that very same day he found an axe and tried to chop down a tree and hit his foot. So that was our first day on the farm."

We shuddered. I said, "If that bullet had hit you, we would not be here either."

"Well, thank God it didn't. Cut a little narrower, Mabel." Once we were back at our tasks, she went on, her story punctuated by the noise of Ray and Leo stacking wood in the porch every few minutes. The sound of saws being filed sometimes was as sweet as a fiddle and other times was so sharp it set my teeth on edge. But as she went on with her story of long ago, I felt content and comfortable with the whole family at home, much cozier and more comfortable than her family had been nearly twenty-five years before.

"That first winter was dark and dreary. Pa started logging right away and Mama took care of the cows. The two workmen stayed on to help with logging and clearing land. They slept on a bunk bed in the kitchen of that two-room cabin."

"Where did you go to school if you were way out in the woods?" I wondered.

"That really worried me when I knew we were going. There was no school anywhere around. Before we left Virginia I told my teacher that, and she wrote a note to the Superintendent of Schools. His name was . . . Lafayette Bliss!"

We giggled as Mother went on. "I went to see him at Roosevelt High School. It was so important to me that I didn't feel a bit nervous, though I was only ten. He gave me as many books as I could carry, and that made me quite happy."

"Quite blissful," I teased.

Mother glanced at the clock. It was nearly dinner time. But she wanted to finish the story.

"That was a lo-o-ong winter. I was still complaining and wanting to go to school, so Pa took me to Pike River to stay with a couple of old friends. They were an old couple with no children, and I had been used to having my brothers and sisters around. Every evening I cried myself to sleep. After two weeks Uncle Christian came to see how I was doing, and *nothing* could keep me there any longer; I *had* to go home."

"That sure does sound boring," said Mabel. "When do we get to the Paradise part?"

"Yes, the cabin was crowded and stuffy, and we had to chop a hole in the ice of the lake for water. Pa used to take the little ones to the *savusauna* by the lake on a homemade sled. We had that, and a barn, and the cabin. There's still a piece of it over Grandpa's root cellar.

"And don't forget, we really were pioneers. There were Indians living in tepees across the lake who were trappers. We were kind of scared of them at first. That first winter, especially, they would stop at our cabin and Mama would give them coffee because they were so cold. No matter how much food she put on the table they ate *every crumb*, and finally she didn't give them anything but coffee because we couldn't afford to, so they stopped coming."

Mabel felt she had missed something wonderful. "Oh, Mother, I'd have liked to see them paddling their canoes and living in their tepees."

Vic called from upstairs, "I think we're getting just as hungry as they were."

Mother called back, "I'm almost through, and then dinner will be on in two shakes of a lamb's tail.

"Spring came, and it was a beautiful spring. Everything brightened up. We burned brush from the land clearing almost every evening, and all of us children piled brush on the fire. It was really like a party for us.

"We had to use all our potatoes for seed, and Mama planted a garden right away. Fortunately it was a wonderful strawberry season. We picked wild strawberries for hours, and had pancakes and strawberries, strawberries and pancakes—with whipped cream—three times a day."

"Yummm," we interjected.

"Of course we also had bread and biscuit, milk, buttermilk, cream and butter, and sometimes fish, and found our meals satisfying.

"As land was cleared, the place opened up. That spring we had company from Virginia, some good friends of my parents. They asked Mama, 'Aren't you lonesome here?' because she had always been such a sociable person. 'It was a hard, lonely winter,' she answered, 'but when Spring came and the leaves were out and the birds were singing, I thought to myself, 'This is Athens, Paradise.' "

The clock struck twelve. Ray and Leo came in ruddy and snowy. Chairs scraped upstairs, saws were put away. Mabel and I pushed aside the boxes of carpet rags and set the table.

Soon Bobby was in his high chair with a mashed-up version of dinner before him. All of us were seated around the table, heartily enjoying roast venison, baked potatoes with gravy, canned green beans, and thick slabs of Mother's special whole-wheat-and-rye bread with a hint of molasses, spread with sweet butter. There was tapioca pudding with blueberry sauce for dessert. As I licked the last delicious morsel from my spoon, I closed my eyes and blissfully declaimed, "*This* is Athens, Paradise."

❈❈❈❈❈❈❈❈❈❈❈

We were snowbound for two more days. The boys shoveled paths to barn and stable, outhouse and garage, and, on Saturday, to the sauna. Mabel and I continued to cut carpet rags and to stitch similar strips together. Mother sat with us when she had time, and rolled the strips into balls while she told us more family history.

Some of her stories were almost too spooky. She often knew who was calling, and with what tragic message, even before the phone rang. Once she put down her scissors when the phone rang—not with our number—carefully took the receiver off the hook, covered the mouthpiece with her hand, and said, "I just know it's the Wiermaa boy." When she hung up she said, "Yes, the poor little thing died of pneumonia."

By Saturday afternoon the storm had passed, and the blue smoke from the sauna rose straight up. Only a film of small snowflakes drifted through the air, a crystal haze across the clearing sky.

"Hey, the snowplow's coming through!" Leo called just as darkness was falling. The yellow monster, its bright headlights gleaming, left high banks as its huge V-shaped blade sprayed a fountain of snow toward each side of the road.

We heard Mother invite the driver to coffee as she came in from milking. She said, "My upper lip itches. Company's coming for sure. Good thing there's some Cousin Jack left."

We hurried with supper, then shook out the rag rugs on the front steps that Ray had scraped free of snow. I swept the floor and Mabel spread out each rug in its proper place. We were washing dishes when a car pulled in.

Weary of being snowbound for days, the Heikki Hiltulas had come to sauna in the wake of the snowplow. They entered saying "God's peace," in the Apostolic Lutheran manner. They had brought their three daughters and left the boys at home.

The men went to sauna at once, while it was good and hot. Mrs. Hiltula sat down in a straight chair and rubbed her back. She was obviously "p.g." Since Nannie Krapu's remarks about Mother's big belly I had become sophisticated enough to notice.

"You really are big this time, Anna," Mother observed. "I bet it's twins."

"*Hyvänen aika*, who needs twins with five already? Well, if God wills it." The soft, tired, pale face behind the round steel-rimmed glasses wore a look of patient resignation.

We took the girls up to our room and showed off our Flossie Flirts—now baptized, with due ceremony, Monica and Marilyn. We played a game of "Button, button, who's got the button?" but soon tired of it. I went downstairs to get some milk for a tea party. I stopped when I reached the landing. The men were back from sauna and the grownups were arguing—something that hardly ever happened with the soft-spoken, gentle Hiltulas.

"Then you don't think it's terrible that the Bolsheviks demand a share of the profits of the co-ops for their party and threaten to break away and establish their own stores if they don't get it?" Mr. Hiltula asked Father.

"We-e-ell, I don't like it," Father slowly replied, "but this is a free country. There's no *Poperikoffi* or *Stalini* to clap us in jail for speaking our minds here. If they want to do it, there's no way to stop them."

Mother spoke more angrily. "Well, *I* think it's *terrible*. We Finns should stick together in something like the cooperative movement. And Communists don't even believe in God."

Mrs. Hiltula didn't join the argument, but as I came downstairs, she was shaking her head sadly. Mother said we'd better get to sauna now, and have our tea party later. Mrs. Hiltula did not feel up to going.

The five of us reveled in a warm, wonderful, soapy bath, along with Mother. "Your water's so soft!" exclaimed Elsie. It makes my hair so clean it squeaks."

"When we saw you coming we took out the rocks and put in feathers," I joked.

After Mother had gone to dry and dress in the dressing room, we threw more cold water on the *kiuas*, making the upper benches unbearably hot; wildly tossed pailfuls of water; commented rudely on various parts of one another's anatomies; and caught one another unaware with splashes of cold water. At first, fifteen-year-old Elsie was uneasily conscious of her plump breasts and pubic hair, but soon joined lustily in the fun.

¤¤¤¤¤¤¤¤¤¤

As usual, it was in bed that I let worries register and bother me. That word—*Comanists*—why did it upset the grownups so much? Now Bolsheviks—that sounded much worse. I'd seen cartoons of wild-eyed, scraggly-bearded men hunched over, about to throw a round black bomb with a lighted fuse. *That* was scary.

I knew there were some Finns who didn't go to church, and whose funerals were conducted by a Unitarian woman minister in Virginia, who obviously couldn't be a Christian. Such Finns ranted about the capitalists, and read the *Työmies*. They must be Comanists. I had heard Mother urge Vic not to listen to the neighbor boy's crazy ideas. Maybe *he* was a Comanist. But then, Father had said this was a free country, so it couldn't be too bad.

I felt my chest. No sign of breasts yet. I soon succumbed to the sweet languor of sauna night.

Vermilion Hall

Miss Sivula appeared determined to make up for all the jollity of December. She required us, more strictly than ever, to learn to spell, write a clear hand—preferably Palmer Method—solve arithmetic problems at various levels of difficulty, and read lessons aloud when we struck a difficult portion in literature or history. When the eighth grade was studying the Middle Ages, she called on Waino Harju to read a paragraph about the feudal system. He paused before one word, then came out with *"pissants."* We glanced mischievously at one another and covered our mouths to stifle our guffaws. Even Teacher's mouth twitched.

She also assigned a lot of memory work: The Gettysburg Address, the Preamble to the Constitution of the United States, and reams of poetry. Each student had to get up in front of the class and recite as much as he could remember. Whether or not it was a fifth grade assignment, I went about, indoors and out, declaiming, "Tell me not, in mournful numbers, Life is but an empty dream," and "If you can keep your head when all about you / Are losing theirs and blaming it on you," as well as romantic ones more to my taste, like Masefield's "I must go down to the seas again, To the lonely sea and the sky," and Edna St. Vincent Millay's "O World, I cannot hold thee close enough!"

Few of the poems we learned in school applied to our ordinary lives. In the lower room we had learned about the world of Robert Louis Stevenson's English childhood—about children with nurses, and lamplighters, and tea time. Now our poetry ranged over big ideas and deep feelings, lofty adventures, heroism, patriotism, love and death. We learned about bravery and death from "Thanatopsis," "O Captain My Captain," and "In Flanders Fields." About love and heartbreak from "Evangeline" and "The Courtship of Miles Standish." I loved the lilt of dancing daffodils, the hoofbeats of "The Highwayman," the rolling alliteration of the barrel organ carolling across a golden street. I never had to be prompted when it was my turn to recite. And I didn't have to worry about carrying a tune.

I *did* have to try not to drive Father crazy, so I confined my elocution as much as possible to my room and outdoors. And largely to please him I learned Finnish poems for Co-op or Farmer's Club programs at the lake or in a park in summer, and at Vermilion Hall in winter.

All year round, in fact, Vermilion Hall was the chief center of community activities. Erected in 1914 by the Socialist Society, it was bought by the Temperance Society two years later and given the more neutral name of the township.

There, groups performed folk dances, classic Finnish plays, comedies, and melodramas that always, it seemed, included a knife fight. Often the mailman brought a postcard announcing a party at Vermilion Hall—a wedding shower, perhaps, or an anniversary celebration, or a fiftieth birthday. Always a P.S. read, "Please bring cake (or cream, or biscuit. . .)"

When the festive evening arrived, the family bundled into the car, often with the exception of Victor, who preferred to see his friends or stay home to bake a cake and perhaps eat half of it before we came home. Babies were laid on the benches around the large lunchroom, divided by a waist-high partition from the meeting and dance hall with its large stage.

While the women prepared the feast, children slid back and forth on the freshly waxed floor, trying to cross it in one swoop. Teenagers usually stayed outdoors in cars or stood in knots in the lee of the hall, until hunger or restless dancing feet drew them in, and they ground out cigarettes and possibly tossed an empty bottle into the woods. The men talked farming and politics while

The Finnish Temperance Hall in nearby Soudan was typical of Finn Halls in many communities.

they waited for coffee.

When the adults were settled around the large U-shaped table, except for three or four aproned women who served the food, a man got up—often Father—and made a complimentary speech suited to the occasion, perhaps with a few jokes bordering on lewdness if it was a wedding shower or anniversary. A bowl was prominently placed in the center of the table, and coins and dollar bills were discreetly dropped into it for the guests of honor. Or the party might be held to raise money for a new stove for the hall, or help a family left fatherless by a mine accident or homeless by a chimney fire that burned down the whole house.

Occasionally the hostesses planned a basket social. Each woman prepared lunch for two and arranged it in a box—perhaps a shoebox from Montgomery Ward—wrapped it in crepe paper as nicely as she could, and decorated it with artificial flowers and ribbons.

With many hints and jokes, a master of ceremonies auctioned off the boxes. Each went to the highest bidder among the men, who then had the privilege of sharing it with the woman whose name he found inside. Many girls let their boy friends know, by some hint, which to bid for; if the others suspected as much, they forced the bid higher and higher. But most partners were surprises, pleasant or not.

Then the dancing began! Matt Mattson, up on stage, played his accordion, often with Charlie Niemi on the fiddle, and on special occasions a pianist as well. Almost everyone danced, even the little girls—mostly polkas, schottisches, and waltzes.

Mabel and I thought Father was the smoothest dancer on the floor, and were thrilled when he came to give one of us a whirl. He was easy to follow, and long before we were ten, we knew all the old-time dances. Mother stayed in the lunchroom gossiping over coffee and tending to Bobby; she had never learned to dance.

The dancers hopped merrily to polkas. The couple who danced fastest and most madly around the floor and ended up flushed and panting were applauded and cheered. They cavorted just as gaily to more modern tunes. But when a waltz was played they moderated their steps to smooth circles round and round the room. I was happiest when Father, with his masterful leading and perfect sense of rhythm, chose me for a waltz. Every so often a "broom dance" was announced. Some unlucky person had to be partner to a straw broom until he could foist it quickly on someone else during an unexpected break in the music and grab his or her partner.

It was at one such party at Vermilion Hall that one phase of childhood innocence—or ignorance—vanished from my life. And I wasn't sure that knowing was really better than wondering, for with information came shock and dismay.

For some reason a small orchestra from Virginia had been hired for this particular party, and played the hit tunes of the day as well as oldies and folk dances. I watched intrigued as Miss Sivula and Eino Salmela danced a rhumba, now and again bending in a graceful arc, Eino's handsome blond head above Miss Sivula's marcelled light brown waves. I had had no idea that my staid teacher could arch her back so beautifully and smile so beguilingly into her partner's eyes. I found that interesting and romantic. But soon I saw everything in a new and different light.

❦❦❦❦❦❦❦❦

After dancing a particularly strenuous polka with Aili, I went to the lunchroom for Kool-Aid and cookies. I heard a woman say, "Of course they had to get married; she was four months 'p.g.'"

I asked Sylvia Koski what that meant—why did they *have* to get married?

"Oh you little dumbbell," she replied from the superiority of eighth-grade status, "it means they did it and she's going to have a baby, but they weren't married so they had to get married. It happens all the time."

"But *what* did they *do?*"

"If I told you, your mother would break my neck."

But I pestered her until she explained, none too subtly, what "doing it" consisted of.

I was stunned. The rest of the evening I watched the couples dancing, some holding each other close, and pictured them "doing it." I looked at the babies and almost hated Mother, first for telling me Mrs. Simonson had brought Bobby, then, after she was aware that I knew they grew inside the mother, not telling me how babies got started. What was so wrong in knowing? People celebrated weddings; they rejoiced when a baby was born. Why were grownups so secretive, as if there were something shameful about it all? Why had I been too dumb and timid to put it all together? When I grew up and got married, I, too would "do it" and have babies. Like all my girl friends, I had played at getting married and having babies; it was natural and expected. But the connection had been left out.

Even now I felt sure it was something Mother wouldn't talk about. Nor could I discuss it with Mabel. She was too small to be burdened with such a sudden earthshaking revelation. Maybe I should tell her carefully and gradually. I pondered it all evening, even in bed, until I fell uneasily asleep, exhausted from more than dancing.

Next day in school, my class work done, I took a sheet of tan construction paper and idly drew a naked man and woman as I imagined they "did it." Teacher was making her silent rounds of the room and stopped beside me with a gasp. She snatched the paper, grabbed one arm in a tight bony grip, dragged me, bewildered and frightened, out into the hall, and banged shut the classroom door.

Through a fog of tears, I gathered that what I had done was *sinful* and *dirty* and I should be *ashamed* of myself.

Never had I had such a hysterical scolding; never had I cried so bitterly. Teacher's face was contorted with anger; she made me look into her eyes, and they seemed to bore into my soul. Her teeth looked enormous, and spit squirted from the sides of her mouth as she raged. Her diatribe over, her voice still shaking, she made me promise never to do such a thing again. I gulped and nodded miserably, my hands rubbing my streaming eyes. "Now go wash your face and come back in when you think you can face me again."

The other children wondered what Teacher's pet could possibly have done to produce such an explosion of anger and such red and swollen eyes. Had she, maybe, drawn a cartoon of Teacher dancing with Eino? Whatever it was, all but a few friends snickered, and when Teacher wasn't looking, they pointed a finger at me and stroked the other forefinger across it toward me and whispered, "Shame, shame, double shame, Everybody knows your name!"

I was thankful that Leo had stayed home with a cold. The bus ride seemed to take hours. When Mother noticed my reddened nose and watery eyes, I said I must be getting a cold, too. She asked if I could finish the churning anyway.

I vented some of my anger and frustration by turning the barrel as hard as I could. The fresh buttermilk soothed my throat, but I didn't want to stay and watch Mother work the butter. I said I had to read a chapter of History, and escaped to my room.

I was too spent to cry any more, but I was still full of anger. I lay on my stomach, kicked the bed and clenched the pillow tightly. I felt robbed not only of knowledge but of some of the mystery of life. Lies had robbed me of them, and I was sure I would never be happy again. I hated everybody, most of all myself.

Troubles and Tears

True enough, I was unhappy for a while. In fact, I remember
that whole spring as pretty miserable.

A few days after Miss Sivula berated me, I was down—
again—with a sore throat and fever. As she applied trusted re-
medies, Mother reminded me of Dr. Malcolm's warning. The
fat old general practitioner at Soudan Hospital had warned that
if I had another sore throat my tonsils would have to come out.

When I was well enough, Father drove us to Soudan. I
meekly climbed on to a narrow table, breathed in sweet and sick-
ening chloroform, and dizzily spiraled down into buzzing noth-
ingness.

When I woke I saw the doctor's ruddy face smiling down
at me. "There, little lady. It's all over. Here's a nickel. An ice
cream cone will make you feel better."

I hurt too much to smile back. After Father had paid him
his ten-dollar fee, I weakly made my way to the car and covered
myself with a blanket. The vanilla cone from Marttila's helped
for a few minutes. I kept spitting blood, but the lingering chloroform made it look unreal and far away.

For a few days I languished and dozed, ate soft custards, fruit soup, milk toast. One day I came downstairs to look at the pictures in the big drawer. I looked longer and harder than ever before at Mother's and Father's wedding picture.

Three young men and three young women gaze out of the yellowed photo. The bride is seated at the groom's left. Her light blue eyes have the same direct look as she had in the pictures of her as a ten-year-old child. Now, at eighteen, she is a grown woman, unsmiling but not sad, her face full and firm. Her dark hair is parted in the middle and tied with a wide ribbon and bow. Her white voile dress allows the lacy edge of a petticoat to peek above a new pair of sturdy high-top shoes. The neckline is modest, but not high. The sleeves come below the elbow. Around her plump shoulders and across her rounded bosom is a wide fichu edged in lace. A spray of three long-stemmed roses follows the line of the left side; the lowest rose and leaf reach her waistband. There are two deep tucks in her skirt. She wears a broad gold band on the third finger of her left hand.

In a week the groom will be 28 years old. He wears a dark suit with a high vest and, like the other men, a long, dark, narrow tie with an ornament at the knot. A heavy watch chain dangles in an arc from his vest to his trousers pocket. A rose hangs, blossom down, from his left lapel. His shiny new boots are buttoned up the side. The collar of his white shirt is narrow and turned down. His face is handsome, chiseled, thin. A carefully trimmed mustache curves away from a well-shaped mouth. His hairline is high, his hair parted on the left and combed into a wave from which a lock separates on his right temple. Like Mother, he seems to be looking into a far distance.

"Mother, how did you happen to meet Father and marry him?"

Mother was feeding the baby chicks huddled on old newspapers around the kitchen range, walled in by the woodbox and window screens. They had come by mail in heavy cardboard cartons with air holes and until the chicken coop was warm enough, we had to put up with their cheeping and mess.

She stood up, eased her back, sat down in the rocking chair, and got that familiar faraway look.

"My upper lip itches. Company must be coming, but I'll just take a minute to tell you before I clean up."

I was so enthralled with her story that many minutes went by. I had heard only bits of it before. We had little time alone together, and she was as willing to talk as I was to listen.

"We were sad after Mother died, but we had to bake and clean and cook and take care of the baby, and in the spring and fall all of us had to pick rocks so the men could plow the fields. So we didn't have time to mope. And we did have fun too.

"Lydia and I often walked the five miles to Peyla to visit our old schoolmates. And we often got together with our Swedish neighbors, the Pearsons, the Johnsons, and the Wahlstens, to play games or have songfests. Lillian Pearson played the organ that we bought from her a few years ago. The Temperance Society had a community hall by the Pike River bridge in Peyla, that's now the church; we had parties like basket socials there. And often on Sundays we met in different homes and went on winter sleigh rides and summer picnics.

"By the time I was seventeen, the Hiltunen brothers, Peter and Arvid, were around. Father told me he saw me wearing a brown tam at the railroad station and thought, 'What a pretty girl.' At one basket social, he got my basket; at another, Arvid did. Both of them acted interested, but I wasn't sure which one I liked better."

"Oh, Mother! Father's much nicer than Uncle Arvid. I mean, he's nice, but I wouldn't want him for a father. He's always sure he knows best."

Mother's smile agreed with me. "Well, on New Year's Eve as 1912 was coming in, I dreamed that I married Peter Hiltunen, and I told Lydia next morning and laughed and laughed at such a silly idea. I had three or four suitors, including the first, Edward Wahlsten. And I liked Arvid better at that time.

"Then in the spring we stayed at Salmelas' for two weeks while we attended confirmation school. Peter was living with a family about a mile away, and we two often went for walks, and we'd stop on the narrow wooden bridge and gaze at the river and talk and we just got so close.

"But mostly all of us young people went bumming from house to house and just had such a good time. The girls scrubbed the hall and decorated it with cedar boughs, and the class was confirmed on April 28."

"Mother, do you ever forget a date? You know *everybody's* birthday."

Not only that, she often started her day mentioning anniversaries of deaths, weddings, community and family events of all kinds, as well as birthdays, over her first cup of coffee.

"By August we had agreed to be married, and when I told Lydia that, she said, 'Now, how about your dream?'"

The mystery of Mother's prophetic New Year's Eve dream made me shiver and hunch my shoulders. After a moment I asked hoarsely, "Were you in love?"

Mother picked up the newspapers Father had left scattered around the rocking chair and began to tidy them into a neat pile. She glanced at me, pondering the answer to a brash nine-year-old's question. "Why, yes, of course we were. I thought he was smart and good—and very good-looking.

"The wedding was set for Sunday, November 10, but the Reverend Hirvi couldn't come that day so it was moved up to the ninth. Mrs. Aho made our dresses. The day before the wedding I was scrubbing the kitchen floor—on my hands and knees, of course—when a blond Finn named Joseph appeared and said, 'Lydia tells me you're cleaning house for your wedding and here I've come to ask you to be my wife.' I had to keep from laughing right out loud, because I'd never even thought of him for two minutes, and it was lucky I had my back to him. I swallowed and said in Finnish, 'I guess that's true.'"

I laughed with her until my throat hurt too much to laugh.

"Did you have a church wedding, Mother?" I croaked.

"No, that wasn't so common in those days when it was hard to get around. Reverend Jacob Hirvi came to Wahlsten's Station by train and Father picked him up in the buggy, and he performed the ceremony about 3:30. Arvid and Heikki Hiltula were his attendants, and Lydia and Hilja Jacobsen were mine. Then we had a good dinner, and a decorated layer cake, and a small but jolly party."

"Peter and Arvid took turns playing the accordion. With Heikki, they sang romantic Finnish songs, like 'It was a lovely summer evening,' and 'Charming maiden, you grew in your father's cabin like a beautiful sweet flower in the grass.' Some people danced; Lydia really whirled in her new pink dress, but I didn't join in."

"Oh, Mother, it's so much fun to dance. Why not?"

"Oh, I guess I was a little shy and then I was always so busy, I just never got started. But oh, how Grandpa enjoyed the party! His eyes just twinkled. I hadn't seen him so happy since Mother died.

"Next morning we took the train to Tower to have this picture taken. Four inches of snow had fallen the night before, but it was a warm day and so our voile dresses got rather wrinkled under our long coats."

She gazed at the picture and shook her head slowly, as if it were hard to believe. "Oh, we were all so young! If I'd realized how different Finns and Americans are . . . Oh, well. Now I'd better get back to work. You know Kirjonen just freshened and I better see how she and the calf are doing."

I sat on holding the picture. They had been married the day before by a minister, so it was all right to "do it" and have babies, even though Mother was only eighteen. And they had a lot of them, six already—one every year at first. I wondered if Mother had liked it. Was she still in love? Did all married people sometimes argue? She looked sweet and serious in the picture. She was really married, but still free of babies and sick kids, and so much work. And she hadn't been "p.g."; Victor was born on their first wedding anniversary.

Father and Mother's wedding picture. Behind them are Henry Hiltunen, Olga Jacobson, Arvid Hiltunen, and Lydia Lempia. They were married on November 9, 1912. This photograph was taken the next day.

She came in laughing. "Mrs. Kyyhkynen"—she drew out the funny name to make me laugh too, though it hurt my throat —"is so mad! She was coming down the lane, and when she saw me she sort of put her head down like this, and pawed the ground with her foot like this, and looked up at me from under her eyebrows, and tied her white scarf tighter under her chin. And she said to me, 'Your bull has gotten into our pasture again.'"

Mother said bull—*sonni*—as if it had several strong "n"s and ended in an explosive snort. She looked so much like an angry bull that I laughed some more.

Just then a car turned into our road. Suddenly Mother gasped at the untidy kitchen. The chicks' sweetish feathery smell, their droppings on newspaper. . . . And Bobby's cheeks were still smeared with oatmeal and milk. The rugs were crooked and bumpy, and newspapers and magazines and seed catalogs were strewn on the table and on the floor around the rocking chair. The table was still full of breakfast dishes, and the floor hadn't been swept.

"Of course it has to be Alice Larson, and somebody with her. When my lip itched I should have been busy cleaning instead of being so lazy." But she smiled quickly at me so I would know she had enjoyed our little talk too.

The county nurse came in, looking like an ad for health tonic. With her was a young cadet nurse with a perky white cap and a neat uniform covered with a navy blue cape lined in red.

I liked Alice, who always seemed to care how we were and never lost her rosy Swedish smile except when she scolded you for forgetting to brush your teeth. But the girl looked around the kitchen as if she couldn't believe real people lived like this. I don't know how I knew; I must have felt her shrink and seen her wrinkle her powdered nose. I felt humiliated.

I wanted to scream at her, "We really aren't pigs. We try hard to keep this house neat, but it's too small for all of us, and we're farmers, not rich city people like you. We haven't had time to clean up yet, and those darn chicks will soon be moved into the coop, and I'm sick and Mother scrubs and works all the time!" The unspoken words caught in my sore throat, along with the sour taste of embarrassment.

Miss Larson explained to the girl, "Mrs. Hiltunen has six children, and this one just had her tonsils out."

She held out a tongue depressor, asked me to say "Ah," and told Mother my throat was still red but I could go back to school in a week. Then she checked Bobby's eyes, ears, and throat, discussed his diet, and pronounced him a fine baby.

As they said goodbye, the girl added, "Very interesting." I felt like a bug she was examining, and held back tears only until the door closed behind them. Why couldn't they have come after we had cleaned up, maybe when there weren't any stinky chicks, or when I was in school and didn't have to see the city girl look around so curiously and hold herself so stiffly and smile so falsely? Some day, I thought, I'd show her—though I wasn't sure just how.

Mother understood. "They sure caught us at a bad time. But never mind. Alice is really nice and kind; she's seen this house looking more the way we like it. You go on up to bed and rest so you'll be ready for school next week."

✿✿✿✿✿✿✿✿✿✿

Rain and the sudden spring thaw brought mud vacation. By the time it was over I was well enough for school—still a bit pale and wobbly but glad the sun was bright again and the roads were dry, and a pale mist of green hung around the trees like a lacy shawl.

The thaw also ended Father's and Vic's lumbering. When the roads were dry enough, Father started his county road job, a political plum in the eyes of envious neighbors. But it was no sinecure. He did earn $60 a month, a welcome addition to his income from farm and woodland. To earn it, however, he sat, dust mask covering his nose and mouth, up high on the grader, a clattering yellow machine that smoothed out winter's ruts and frost bumps from the secondary gravel roads, for long hours every clear day.

This job, his income from logging and a loan from Uncle Arvid enabled him to buy a 1930 Model A Ford, a nice new one with windows that rolled up and down instead of the old car's bothersome side curtains of crackly yellowish celluloid and stubborn snaps.

Perhaps to protect his investment, he rewarded Victor for his winter's work with a car of his own—a 1921 Model T roadster, as well as a blue serge suit for confirmation—price, $7.50. All that spring and summer, Vic and Ray worked on that car in their free time during the week, and drove it madly on weekends.

When they went out to dances and movies, nothing would do but freshly ironed white shirts and neatly pressed trousers. I was persuaded, for a small fee, to turn them out neat enough even for fussy Ray. I had to remember to dampen the shirts with the ketchup bottle with a sprinkler cap attached to a cork, at least an hour before ironing them, so they would be evenly damp. I had already learned to iron my own dresses. Manipulating the three sadirons in turn was tricky; as I clamped a new one into the holder I tested it very carefully lest I scorch the cloth, and it seemed no time at all before it was too cool to do the job. No wonder we never seemed to reach the bottom of the ironing basket.

Anyway, with Father's job, the new cars, and another lovely spring beginning, life was good once more.

᠅᠅᠅᠅᠅᠅᠅᠅᠅

Mrs. Hiltula did have twins, as Mother had predicted. The girl was normal and healthy, but the boy was a blue baby and lived only a few days. One glorious May afternoon, school was dismissed so the children could attend his funeral at the Apostolic Lutheran Church about a quarter of a mile up the river road. I walked happily arm in arm with Aili, the sickness and disgrace of late winter forgotten in the beauty of the day. Until I entered the gloomy old log church, where Mother had gone to school twenty years before, my mood remained buoyant.

We filed past the tiny coffin near the altar. We sniffled and wiped our eyes as we turned back to sit down in the pews. The cold waxen blue figure in white ruffles, its tiny fingers curled and bony, was dead. Dead. My throat began to hurt again.

Then I lifted my head to look at the minister in amazement. What was he saying? That we are all born in sin and condemned to Hell unless we repent and live according to the gospel. I had heard all that before. But this was a tiny baby's funeral. How could that red-faced ranting apply to him?

The minister lowered his voice and tenderly said that this baby was lucky. He died in all innocence, baptized and free of any chance to sin. He was to be envied; he was in Heaven now with the angels.

The pastor drew out the word "angels"—*enkelit*— and "in Heaven"—*taivaassa*—smoothly and sanctimoniously. Then he began to shout once more. "Let this innocent babe be an example to all of you sinners. It could be any time—any minute—if not today, then tomorrow. But the awful day of judgment will come."

His face grew redder, his voice hoarser. He chopped the air and banged the pulpit with his hairy fists.

"Let us pray." Again his voice was syrupy and mellow, his words drawn out as if to spread a soothing balm on our bruised and blackened souls. But I wasn't soothed. I could hardly wait to leave the cold unfriendly church for the bright afternoon. Even the beautiful words of the benediction, which usually seemed to bestow a special blessing on me, only made me more impatient. As soon as it was over, I dashed out the door and ran to the road, sobbing.

Sivia and Aili came running after me. "What's the matter? Are you sick again?"

I gasped, "Oh, the poor baby!" and went on sobbing. How could I tell them how angry I was? That pastor had never said, "What a shame, how sorry I am, that this child never had a chance to live." No. He had said he was glad the baby died. I knew by now how mothers suffered to bring babies into the world. I was sure Mrs. Hiltula couldn't be glad. Babies were a lot of work and worry, but they were cute and sweet, and it was fun to watch them grow up into different kinds of people. I thought of how much pleasure Bobby had given all of us.

The girls held me around the shoulders and kept saying, "Mavis, stop crying. It's not *your* brother."

But I couldn't begin to explain; it didn't even occur to me that an Apostolic Lutheran and a non-churchgoer were both trying to comfort me.

I felt only that life was miserable enough; we should be helped over our sorrow and pitied for our weakness, and reassured about life and Heaven. I deserved better of God than to have my first perfect spring day after weeks of shame and humiliation and pain spoiled by a threatening sermon over a tiny body in a pathetic little coffin. Maybe Jesus loved me, as Mother had taught us to sing, but I couldn't believe in the minister's cruel God. The God who had made this May afternoon wouldn't rejoice at the death of a little baby or threaten me with hellfire.

But I didn't dare talk about it, even if I could have said it clearly. I would have to pretend, as I did in so many other situations. Everyone else seemed to take such things in stride, as a matter of course. I dared not appear too different. I wiped away my tears and started to skip along the road, hand in hand with my friends.

A few evenings later, not long after the school bus dropped us off, the teachers came walking down the road. Mother had asked them to supper. Most families invited them once a year, but Mother invited them oftener. She knew they must be lonely on long weekends in the teacherage, when they had so much work to do that they couldn't go home—correcting papers, decorating classrooms, making bulletin boards, filling out report cards, perhaps staying for a school or community function. She knew, too, that they felt comfortable with her because she spoke such good English and prepared such good and hearty meals. And Father or one of the boys would drive them back after dark.

Miss Sivula was all smiles, as if my disgrace had never been. I tried to be inconspicuous—no clowning, no riddles, no jokes. Mother had the downstairs rooms as clean and neat as she could get them with whatever help we had time for after school. As I looked around, with the soft sunset light streaming into the window of the other room, I wished Miss Larson had brought that stuckup girl on a day like this. Everything smelled good. The chicks had long since been banished to the chicken coop.

Teachers Mabel Sivula and Ada Nikkinen with Bobby, May 1931.

The floor was freshly scrubbed and swept and the bright rag rugs were freshly washed and straight. Windows gleamed. Curtains were crisp and white. Newspapers and magazines were tucked up on the Little Floor, out of sight. Bobby was dressed in a little white shirt with short navy blue pants that buttoned on to it.

"How do you manage, Mrs. Hiltunen?" asked Miss Nikkinen. "Your house is always spick and span."

Mother stifled a laugh as she looked at me, and said, "Well, it sometimes gets pretty messy."

Over our blueberry pie, Miss Nikkinen smiled teasingly at Miss Sivula. "Mabel, don't you have some important news for us?"

Miss Sivula blushed, swallowed hard, and then smiled brightly. "I won't be coming back next year. I'm going to marry Elmer Sundstrom."

Perhaps to cover up her blushes and put a stop to our exclamations, she went on, "But before I leave, I want to be sure to tell Mavis one thing. She really should aim to be a writer. And I'm sure you'll see that she gets to college, Mr. and Mrs. Hiltunen."

❀❀❀❀❀❀❀❀❀❀

Again, June meant fun and freedom, work and play, and Bible School. When the Model T was working, we all crowded in, Leo perched daringly on the running board, to drive the two miles to School 40. On Confirmation Day, we all dressed in our best for the important rite that somehow would confer adult status on Victor and Ray.

Rev. Aho catechized the little group of confirmands. Often he failed to get a correct answer until he turned to Vic.

The rite of incorporation as full members of the Evangelical Lutheran Church over, the girls sat in chairs on the lawn, the boys behind them, Reverend Aho seated center front, to have their photo taken. The boys looked young and solemn in their unaccustomed suits, white shirts and ties. The girls also looked serious in their white dresses and stockings and neat black shoes. Their hairdos, all alike except for color and curl, were parted on the left and cut into bangs. No one was more serious than the pastor himself. Confirmation was a solemn rite of passage, not to be diminished by frivolity.

Uncle Ray recalled one occasion when the solemn mood had been broken. He teased Mabel. "When Reverend Aho was asking all those questions, I expected you to ask your father, 'Doesn't the *pappi* know anything?' the way you did when you were about three."

He laughed, remembering how her clear voice had sounded through the little church. Father's tenor laugh had burst out, and the sedate congregation rocked with laughter until even the minister smiled. Mabel hit Uncle Ray's arm and hid her blush in Father's chest.

Father tried to comfort her. He hugged her and said, "Never mind, *Meiboli*, it was funny then, and one of these years we'll forget it."

Not one to pout for long, she went to the kitchen to see if the goodies that went with coffee were ready. Uncle Ray called her back so he could take a picture of all the Hiltunens together.

That ritual over, Ray and Vic ignored the coffee social on the lawn, went straight to the Model T, cranked it up and drove away—proclaiming, at least this once, their newly-won adulthood and freedom.

Confirmation, Sunday, June 1930. Left to right: Mabel, Mavis, Leo, Ray, Mother with Bobby in her arms, Father and Victor.

Juhannus Juhlat

The weekend nearest St. John's Day—*Juhannus*, June 24—
thousands of Finns from all over the Iron Range gathered, now in
one town, the following year in another, to celebrate a festival—
a *juhla*. This day of St. John the Baptist had become the traditional
celebration of the beauty of Midsummer. Father and Uncle Arvid
had told us that in Finland they helped build enormously high
kokkos or bonfires, and stayed up all that white night, when the
sun never sank below the treetops, to dance and make merry.

In late June, 1929, about 10,000 Finns and Finnish Americans gathered in Ely, that jumping-off place into the Superior
National Forest, that rough mining and lumbering town which
the fiery evangelist Billy Sunday said differed from Hell in only
one respect: a railroad ran into Ely. For two days good will pre-
vailed. Religious and political differences were forgotten and
we were all Finns together.

"How come we're going to stay all night at Aunt Lydia's? I
hate to sleep on the floor," Mabel protested.

Father took "his girl" on his lap and said, "It would be too
late to drive home after the banquet and the play tonight, and

149

you have to get some sleep, even on the floor, so you can hear *Vikki* and *Reino* and your *Isä* sing tomorrow."

We left Miina Anderson tending to the milk and the breakfast dishes, and piled into the Ford. Crowded on the edge of the back seat between the boys, Mabel and I clutched the front seat and peered out to see the sights along the twenty-mile trip. Tower and Soudan were familiar enough, but then came the scary curves of the road to Ely. The sun shone warm and bright on lakes and forests, on the "mountain" of Jasper Peak, on the rock-crushing plant near a quarry. We read the cigarette billboards showing a fat future looming behind a slim lady, and the warning, "Coming Events Cast Their Shadows Before - Reach for a Lucky Instead of a Sweet." Ray nudged me and whispered, "Watch out for all that potato soup this summer."

"Okay, I'll reach for a Lucky instead," and I pretended to wave a long slim cigarette holder the way the movie stars did.

We went first to Aunt Lydia's to tend to Bobby and use the indoor toilet, listen for the sound of the sea in the conch shell, rattle the glass bead curtains between the hall and living room, stroke her satin pillows and sneak a glance at *True Confessions* when Mother wasn't looking. We had plenty of time. We were always early.

"Let's go out and play catch," said Walter. A blonde girl watched us from the porch next door and soon joined us. Walter introduced us casually. "My cousins Mavis and Mabel; my neighbor Helen Anderson."

I felt shy and awkward. She acted very sure of herself. She wore a pretty, obviously "store-bought" organdy dress, and her hair was shiny and curly. Worst of all, she used words I didn't understand. When I timidly admired her dress, she said, "Yeah, Mom bought me some keen clothes for summer." Walter hissed in my ear, "Keen means swell, you dummy."

Helen asked us in for "skaff," which turned out to be coffee. It didn't take me long to decide that I wanted to be just like her and have her for my city friend, to brag about at school. She seemed the height of sophistication, especially because she knew only a few words of Finnish, though her parents had come from Finland.

Mrs. Anderson came into the kitchen and said, "You vant saaklet cake?" I said nothing; I wasn't sure whether I should answer in Finnish or English. Helen said disgustedly, "I've told you many times, Mom, that word is *chocolate*."

We walked along the city streets toward the park. Several

boys about our age laughed and sniggered as they approached and said, "Dumb Finlanders." Helen and Walter retorted, "Dirty *bušuš.*"

We knew Finns weren't any dumber than anyone else—in fact, Walter was probably the smartest kid in Ely. At the moment I was too charmed with Helen to realize she had no reason to be ashamed of her mother just because she wasn't fluent in English.

And the strange boys weren't dirty. But in the little towns of the Iron Range, name calling was part of life—of growing up and identifying with one group and rejecting another.

The Finns we knew called Slovenians, Austrians, and other East Europeans *"bušuš."* When I asked Mother why, she said, "Oh, it doesn't mean anything bad; I guess it's just that their language sounds strange to us, sort of like *bušubušušbušu.*"

༄༅༄༅༄༅༄༅༄

The track and field events and the ball game took place that afternoon. We watched Ray win the pole vault and the high jump, and place second in the hundred-yard dash. We ran toward the ball field when we heard loud cheers, and jumped up and down when we saw Leo crossing third base for a home run.

Folks our parents' age and older sought chairs and benches in the shade and gathered in clusters to exchange news and gossip that might be almost a year old. But we braved sunburn so we could move around to see and be seen, and show off our new city friend and meet her friends. We practiced our new words and phrases: "keen," "Oh yeah?" "Dry up and blow away," "My eye!" and "My foot!" and felt very citified. We ate hot dogs and drank strawberry pop. Sometimes we shook it so hard it fizzed and tickled our noses; the trick was to get it to your mouth before it overflowed.

There was a banquet that night, followed by a play and folk dancing. Mother insisted she would rather stay with Bobby. Aunt Lydia, handsome in her reddish permanented hair and her makeup, scoffed. Her dark eyes flashed as she said, "Come on, Sophie, you hayseed. This is a good chance to get out and have a good time. You don't have to stay for the dance, but you can betcha I will."

"Well, okay, maybe I'll go see the play, but then I'll come

home. I like the comedies and folk dances, but I hope this play isn't full of *puukko* fights."

Walter stayed home with us to look after his little sister Delores while we took care of Bobby. When they were in bed, we looked at stereopticon slides, played card games Walter taught us, and exchanged insults.

Sunday was the Big Day. All morning little boys ran and older people strolled down to the lake and watched barnstormer "Dusty" Rhodes land and take off, again and again, in his little seaplane, giving rides for $3.00. Vic and Uncle Felix jauntily flourished the money and each in turn waved to us as he stepped on the pontoon and then climbed into the front cockpit. Mabel and I watched apprehensively, and were very proud when first Uncle Felix, then Vic, landed and stepped out with a huge grin. Uncle Felix echoed most of the other passengers: "Boy O Boy, that was really something!"

"Geez, Uncle Felix, that was keen," I said.

Not to be outdone, Mabel chimed in, "You looked swell way up there."

We repeated our practice of Ely slang when Vic landed.

At noon the sweating food committee managed to serve *pujaa*—chicken and vegetable stew—to 10,000 people, who had brought their own dishes and silver. They stood in long patient lines, rosy and laughing, joking, exclaiming when they saw old friends, filling one another in on news of births and deaths and marriages. Then they sat at long picnic tables to eat. When they had soaked up the last of the broth with thick slices of bread and had drunk the last sip of coffee, they found seats for the afternoon program—the "cultural events."

The mixed chorus sat on an improvised outdoor stage. Vic and Ray looked very young and solemn in their confirmation suits among the two dozen other men and forty women. Before the conductor appeared, we appraised the women. Marcelled hair peeked from beneath their cloche hats. Skirts barely touched their knees, clad in pinkish silk stockings. The younger ones wore strapped black Mary Jane type shoes; the older ones, sturdy Enna Jetticks like Mother's.

Stout, short Emil Bjorkman stepped to the podium, bowed, stroked his graying mustache and smiled through steel-rimmed glasses in thanks for the applause. The chorus stood. Bjorkman raised his arms, and energetically, with no allowances for its difficulty, he led them through the "Star Spangled Banner," which some of the audience also attempted.

In contrast, there was nothing shaky and uncertain about the way almost everyone joined in the Finnish national anthem, "*Oi Suomen Maa.*" They sang with lovely harmony and great fervor, whether or not they had ever seen the *kukkulat* and *laaksot* of their ancestral land.

After these introductory anthems, the master of ceremonies introduced the governor of Minnesota— a *toiskielinen* who knew quite well, Vic had reminded us, how many of his constituents were Finns. Perhaps he and his predecessors had delivered much the same message before. He greeted the audience in a few halting Finnish phrases, then paid the usual tribute to Finnish *sisu*, told the usual jokes about the sauna, and made the usual bow to the fact that only Finland had paid her World War I debt to the United States. He also told us something we had never learned in school, and I was suddenly riveted by his words.

"You can be very proud," he intoned, "of the fact that Finns helped establish this great country of ours. The man who cast the deciding vote to approve the Declaration of Independence was John Morton. His great-grandfather was Martti Marttinen, born in 1606 in Rautalampi, and his grandfather came to Delaware with that first group of Finnish settlers."

Helen and Walter were whispering. I hissed to them to shut up as the governor went on. "And you probably know," he said, "but I wonder how many other Americans know, that our first President was a Finn!" He waited for the murmur of disbelief to die down.

"Yes, indeed, long before the Constitution was approved and George Washington was elected, our country was administered under the Articles of Confederation. And who held the office of President? John Hanson, another descendant of the earliest Finnish immigrants."

The applause was deafening. His re-election was assured, at least on the Iron Range.

The rest was anticlimax. Announcements, a recitation or two, and then more songs from the chorus—the long vowels and rolling "r"s of the Finnish language softly building up to a conclusion with a shout that almost lifted me off the grass where I sat. A benediction in the reverent tones of Pastor Aho. Applause, pushing aside of chairs, reaching for handbags and coats—for despite the hot day, evenings can be chilly so far north—and with hasty goodbyes, thousands of people headed for their cars and the winding road, the cows waiting at home or the radio and reading lamp in their comfortable city living rooms.

Mother never once scolded Father about taking the curves too fast; we were in a caravan of cars, and she was eager to get home. Besides, she and Father were sharing a precious moment of family unity. Their errant oldest son's bass voice had joined the chorus of patriotism and Finnishness as heartily as Father's and Ray's tenors.

Every few minutes Leo mentioned his home run. The younger children were blissfully smeared with soda pop and ice cream, and after a few excited reminiscences, we drowsed all the way home, resting first on one crowded shoulder, then another, as Father took the sharp curves. He and the boys sang some of the chorus songs, and the festival mood continued in our nice new car. I kept thinking of how wonderful it was to be a Finnish American and how much I would like to live in town and wear store-bought clothes. "Gee whiz, that would really be keen," I whispered to myself.

The Mail Order Bride

It could have been the summer of 1929 that Matt Mattson came home with a mail-order bride. Or it could have been earlier. My memories of many events of my childhood blur into what I've heard over the years from others in the family. Vic has told me his version of Matt's venture into matrimony so often that it seems I remember it too.

Bicycle, home brew, and accordion weren't enough to keep Matt happy. He watched the Personal ads in *The Farmer* and his friend Charlie Hill wrote the answers for him. Perhaps after a little practice and some disappointments they learned to write a convincing reply. At any rate, one day a mail-order bride arrived by train from North Dakota.

I imagine her as a stout, plain woman who had nursed her German immigrant parents through their last illnesses, and found herself at 30 alone on a prairie farm they had bequeathed to her brother. Maybe her Personal ad ran something like this: "Clean home-loving girl invites letters from marriage-minded man." And Matt's replies, courtesy of Charlie, may have convinced her that he owned his own house, was a hard-working,

The kind of bachelor's cabin to which the mail order bride was brought.

cheerful musician, and was looking for a clean, home-loving bride. No one now alive remembers her name. I'll call her Gretti.

Charlie must have been a good liar. Matt bought no more than half a dozen 2¢ stamps—and perhaps sent her a copy of his old passport picture—before she wrote that he should meet her at the train in Tower on a certain day.

That morning Matt turned up before breakfast and asked Vic to drive him to town in the Model T. He looked remarkably clean. He'd worked long and hard making hay the day before, and then had a sauna and bicycled to Charlie Niemi's for a haircut. His blue chambray shirt matched his eyes. New red suspenders held up the thick woolen pants he wore winter and summer, tucked into gray wool socks and laced-up boots. His shy grin alternated with a thoughtful look. I suppose he felt a little apprehensive.

Matt hadn't told us exactly what was up, but Mother was intuitive, and she "had a feeling" he'd bring home a wife. But when they turned up in midafternoon, having stopped by a justice of peace on the way, she was astonished that Gretti knew not a word of Finnish. She wondered how they could communicate, given Matt's rudimentary and broken English.

Matt was beaming. Gretti look confused and bewildered, and ready to cry. Her face lit up when Mother spoke English to her, and she ate ravenously of the good things Mother served with coffee. Then they trudged off over the brook and across the meadow.

Mother watched them go. "That poor girl had no idea what she was getting into. I don't give them six months. No, if it lasts even six weeks, I'll put a cross on the wall."

Vic lost no time calling his friends with the news. They let the newlyweds alone that night, but next evening just before dark, several carloads of young men and teenage boys drove into our yard. They all carried pans, pails, washboards, metal spoons, or short crowbars. I demanded that Vic tell me why.

"That's for the shivaree. I told Ray to go over and put straw under the mattress yesterday while we were in town, and now we're going to give them an old-fashioned shivaree. You'll find out what that is. Just wait."

The men waxed boisterous, possibly because of the moonshine someone dispensed from a car parked well away from the house. But they quieted down once it was dark enough to drive off to the end of the road and slip along the path to Matt's cabin.

Soon we heard unearthly yelling and banging, and Mother said, "That's the shivaree." Matt finally appeared at the door, Vic remembers, pulling his red suspenders over his meaty shoulders and grinning good-naturedly at the visitors. He must have expected them. No older couple escaped a shivaree, and it was best to grin and bear it and thus avoid another hazing.

The pranksters yelled, "Gretti! Gretti!" until she too, appeared, looking even more bewildered than she had the day before; but she managed a friendly smile. Matt passed out nickels and dimes. Finally the gang left, turning occasionally to razz the newlyweds with a raucous yell or risqué remark.

❧❧❧❧❧❧❧❧❧❧

On my tenth birthday Mother let Mabel and me walk to Grandpa's house to visit Aunt Hilma, the redhaired aunt we thought was so glamorous. We were even more charmed after going to get the mail and bringing back a small heavy box, because it contained tubes of oil paint with exotic labels: Viridian Green, Burnt Siena, Cobalt Blue—and Vermilion, which we hadn't known meant a beautiful shade of red. We insisted that Hilma paint a picture at once.

I had been reading a Rafael Sabatini story in one of her magazines—probably the old *Cosmopolitan*. She decided to copy the picture of Captain Blood, and we watched, fascinated, as his face and figure, sword in hand, emerged on the heavy cardboard she used as a canvas. Now this was romantic—a beautiful redheaded aunt painting a dashing swashbuckling hero. I told her so and added, "I s'pose Matt thinks he and Gretti are romantic—but Ish!"

It was too hot to play outdoors. We cranked up the old Victrola and listened to Enrico Caruso's songs and a scratchy record of the Two Black Crows swapping lines in Negro dialect.

Soon after coffee time, Hilma's boyfriend drove up in his Ford coupe, and we were thrilled to sit in the rumble seat when he drove us home. They stopped to visit for only a few minutes. John took Hilma's arm as they went back to the car, helped her in and closed the door. As they drove away I stood rapt in dreams of being nineteen and beautiful. Then I saw the first evening star. I murmured,

> "Star light, star bright,
> First star I see tonight,
> I wish I may, I wish I might
> Have the wish I wish tonight."

I crossed my fingers and made a wish. I longed to be a lovely auburn-haired maiden, a talented painter (or perhaps a writer?) swept into a gleaming carriage by a dashing swordsman and carried off into the sunset.

❦❦❦❦❦❦❦❦❦❦

Soon Mother had something new to worry about. Vic became a hobo.

Tramps had sometimes come to our door and offered to do chores for a meal or a night's lodging. The boys often mimicked them (perhaps after a longish absence or a foolish misdeed), leaned against the door jamb, and asked in a low growl as if embarrassed to beg, *"Saako tässä talossa olla yötä?"* (Can I stay in this house for the night?) Word had apparently got around in the wandering brotherhood that the Hiltunens were hospitable and their food was good.

Mother had read in the papers about the hordes of young men who rode the freights and tramped the roads. But when Vic and his buddy Wallace Ollilla took a notion, right after hay-making time was over, to follow the Western harvest, that was different. This was her fifteen-year-old son, who had plenty to eat and a good clean bed. She pleaded with him to forget the idea, but he thirsted for adventure and wanted to be part of the scene, and one morning his bed was empty.

Mother was a champion worrier. I could read her thoughts as she worked over the butter bowl, sang more hymns than ever while she milked the cows, and sighed as she rocked the baby. She looked down the road every little while as if she expected someone.

I was no slouch at worrying either. Mabel and I sometimes worked ourselves into a crying jag. We imagined Vic among un-shaven bums, sleeping on the ground under a bridge and cooking mulligan stew in a tin can like the the tramps in the funny papers —or worse yet, going hungry. But precious August days were not to be wasted in fretting, and most of the time we roamed woods and fields, picked berries and flowers, and played hide-and-seek with visiting children. We shouted and listened for the echo from the woods across the meadow. We paddled in the brook and chased fireflies as twilight deepened.

⚙⚙⚙⚙⚙⚙⚙

One sunlit evening Mother disappeared. When we got up from the supper table she was nowhere to be seen. Bobby was crying. Father picked him up and asked us to change his diaper and then look for Mother. I ran to the toilet and the chicken coop, Mabel to the sauna and barn. The berry patches across the brook, on the Little Hill, and along the lane to Krapus' were deserted. The farm felt desolate without Mother's solid presence.

I ran up on the wooded hill behind the house and found her sitting under a tall Norway pine, leaning back against its trunk. She looked at me as if she hardly knew me and didn't like me very much. I was dismayed. "Mother, what's the matter?"

"I'm just tired. I'm so tired. Everyone else can run around and go visiting and have a good time. Victor used to notice if I needed help with the cows and the baby and the garden, but no one was around at milking time, not even to take care of Bobby." She clutched her blue calico apron to her face and sobbed. "I am so tired of everything."

I cried too. She took me into her lap and wiped my face with her apron. "Oh, Mother, I'm sorry. I'll help you more. Honest. Cross my heart and hope to die."

Mabel stood a little way off, wide-eyed and wondering. We had never seen Mother in a weak and tearful and self-pitying mood before. She ran to us, kissed Mother, and fervently promised that she would help more too.

Mother sighed, got heavily to her feet, and took our hands to walk home through the stubble on the hillside. She never let us see her so downhearted again. And—at least in spurts—we tried to help her more. It was too easy to forget, when haymaking time was over, that all her chores went on as before.

The long shadows of summer from the pines around the house.

One evening, about three weeks after Vic left, when the shadows of the pines were long and cool, Mother came from the barn with a brimming pail of milk in each hand. A tramp approached along the lane to Krapus' and stooped to slip through the poles that served as a gate. Mother watched. She looked harder at the shabby, dirty scarecrow, whose eyes gleamed white from a grimy face. It split into a wide grin. "Hello, Maw."

She screamed, "Victor!" and dropped her milk pails on the packed earth of the barnyard. I don't think she would have cared if they had spilled. She enfolded him in her soft warm hug and sobbed, "Oh, Victor, I prayed for you. I knew you'd come home safe and sound."

Father and the other boys were still eating supper. While Mabel ran to put more wood on the sauna fire, I loaded a plate with food. We all laughed at Bobby's cringing refusal to let the strange apparition pick him up. After he'd scrubbed his face and hands at the wash stand, Vic sat down to eat and tell his story between bites.

"We rode the freights, of course, like everyone else. We got a job in North Dakota shocking oats and stacking the farmer's third crop of alfalfa. He was a big Swede. He gave me a team of horses to drive that pushed a buck rake. They were so huge I had to stand on a stool or box to reach high enough to get the harness on.

"We ate in the house with the family but we slept in the hay barn. We ate pretty good and slept like a bump on a log because we were so tired. But that job didn't last long. We went to Devil's Lake looking for more work, but the farmers said they weren't getting enough for their crops and couldn't pay workers, so we rode the boxcars home."

Sauna-fresh and dapper, Ray teased Vic. "I've been driving the Model T since you left and I'm going to a barn dance tonight. Wanna come?"

"No, I've danced around enough barns for a while. I just want to soak in the sauna and hit the hay. Glad it's not real hay. Maw, how's Matt doing with that mail order?"

✖✖✖✖✖✖✖✖✖

Next day we found out. Gretti walked over the meadow alone, carrying her suitcase, and found Mother weeding the garden. She squatted down between the carrots and beets and talked earnestly and tearfully for a long time.

She left that very day; Vic drove her to the Tower depot. She had told Matt she wanted to visit her relatives for two or three days and fetch some more of her things. But Mother was right; she had hefted the suitcase and after they left she said, "That's too heavy for a two-day visit. We won't be seeing her again."

It hadn't lasted even six weeks, and no one was surprised, least of all Mother. Now no one remembers just what she looked like, not even her real name. We might wonder for a brief moment what she did with the rest of her life. And, if she lived to be old, what memories of Matt and Minnesota survived the years.

※※※※※※※※※

One chilly evening at the end of August we loaded old quilts and horse blankets into the car and drove to Grandpa's to watch the meteor showers we called shooting stars. For an hour or so, we lay on blankets on the grass, huddled together for warmth, and gazed at the sky.

The grownups summed up the summer. Mother told about Matt's mail-order bride. Father told Grandpa how he'd shot the first buck of the season. Uncles Ray and Felix shared their sorrow over the death of Big Matt Avikainen, deep underground, trapped under a fall of rock so heavy it flattened his miner's lamp to a quarter-inch thickness.

Vic recounted his hoboing adventure. He added, "The more I think about it, the more I feel sure there's going to be a big economic depression. The farmers out West sure think so. Prices for their crops have fallen a whole lot already." No one commented on his gloomy prediction.

Mabel and I snuggled up to Aunt Hilma, sniffed her "Evening in Paris" perfume and asked her about John in a whisper.

Every little while we all exhaled a delighted "Ooh" as a brilliant star streaked across the sky and fell to the horizon. I didn't believe that every falling star was a dying person's soul going to Heaven. It didn't make sense that more people should die during the August meteor showers than at any other time of year.

Still, the thought made me shiver, and I was glad when Aunt Hilma noticed and said, "It's getting too cold to watch any more. Time for coffee."

Potatoes, Blueberries, and Illegal Venison

And so it went for about two more years. Vic pulled away and came back. The family scattered for games and work and sports and school, then gathered for meals and festivals and ordinary home routines. I watched myself grow. I draped scarves or dress lengths around my naked body and assumed one pose after another in front of the mirror. My mind was growing, too. I learned enough about things that had puzzled and worried me when I was eight and nine to understand what grownups argued about so vehemently as we moved into the decade of the thirties.

The October 1929 crash was not devastating to subsistence farmers like us. Father often reminded us, as we sat around the supper table, that many city people were going cold and hungry because they were out of work.

"But *meikäläiset*," he said, "have always been poor. We've lived on what our work could wrest from the fields and woods."

"Yeah," wisecracked Ray, "potatoes, blueberries, and illegal venison."

Father grinned and went on. "And we aren't at the mercy of city stores. We own our own consumer cooperatives."

The co-op. Leo managed the Brimson Co-op in the 1950s and 1960s.

Father was worried, however, about the future of the co-op movement. I heard him talking to visitors, and at meetings and parties. Voices often rose and faces got red, and the word "Communist" had become a topic of everyday discussion.

He asked me to come along with him to a meeting of stockholders of the two-store Embarrass Co-operative Association so that I could help him write up a report for the *Co-op Builder*. I had begun to take my busy mother's place as his secretary, writing up minutes of meetings at the kitchen table, often translating into English when he was stuck for a word. But this was a meeting of Finns, and in Finnish he was eloquent as he warned of the danger.

"Since last July the Communist Party, in the name of The Finnish Workers Federation, has been demanding thousands of dollars, and a share in running the cooperatives. But if they get *any* control,"—he looked seriously at everyone assembled and spoke strongly and persuasively—"if they get any control, they will be militantly political. They will destroy our neutrality.

"It's bad enough that many *toiskieliset* call our co-ops not only 'Finn stores' but 'Red stores.' We must not forget when we founded them in self-defense against gouging merchants who wouldn't give striking miners or unemployed workers credit, we included Church Finns and Temperance Finns and Socialist Finns and even Communist Finns, but we stayed out of politics. And we must continue to be neutral. Otherwise we will be considered dangerously un-American. We must vote down the Communists at the general meeting."

He stayed calm despite hecklers, and then allowed the opposition to state its views. One man argued, "Only if we line up with the workers of the world and fight the capitalists will we ever have any power. The co-operative movement in Europe allows factions to participate in decisions. Why not include the Finnish Worker's Federation as one faction in the cooperative movement?" Hostile murmurs were heard from all sides, and he grew angry, and shouted, "Down with the capitalists! Workers of the world, unite! You have nothing to lose but your chains."

Father, as chairman of the board, stood and calmly waited for the hubbub to die down, and then called for nominations of delegates to attend the general meeting. He was chosen to head the delegation and cast the local association's vote against the Communists. After one brief argument, he and Vic steered clear of the subject.

As he prepared to attend that meeting in Superior, Wisconsin, in April of 1930, Mabel and I felt his excitement, and Mother's, and helped him get ready. After sauna the night before the meeting, he asked me to clip the hair from his nose and ears. I shivered as he pared his nails with his pocket knife. He called for his little bottle of corn medicine and touched his corns with the evil-smelling liquid to soften them before he cut them. Mabel gave him a massage, walking up and down his back on her knees.

Early next morning Mother pressed his trousers and cleaned his felt hat while he shaved with special care. Mabel helped him button his fresh white shirt and straighten his suspenders, and I held his sleeve garters and helped him adjust them so his cuffs came to just the right place. Then he slipped his tie—which, despite Ray's protests, he never unknotted—over his head and looked in the mirror as he adjusted it. Mother helped with his suit coat, and smoothed the shoulders affectionately.

"*No niin.*" He patted his pockets for car keys and billfold, and it seemed he was already at the meeting; his thoughts were not with us long enough to say Goodbye. He must have remembered that, for he tooted the horn as he pulled away.

It was already dark when he came home and flopped into

the rocking chair. Leo was asleep, exhausted from helping clear land for a baseball field. Ray and Vic were upstairs doing homework for the tenth grade in the Embarrass school to which Vermilion ninth- and tenth-graders were bussed. They didn't come down, but their silence was a listening one.

While Mabel untied Father's shoes and took them off, he gave Mother a weary grin and said, "*No niin.* It was a noisy meeting but we won. When the Communists couldn't take over the Co-ops, they walked out. If they open their own stores, that won't hurt us."

᪄᪄᪄᪄᪄᪄᪄᪄᪄᪄

In their spare time, especially during summer vacation, Vic and Ray tinkered with the model T and drove it merrily on weekends. One day when Vic was setting the coils, Ray turned the big hand crank, and it kicked so violently that his forearm was broken.

"*Isä,* come quick!" Vic yelled. Father ran out of the house, saw the sharp ends of broken bone just under the skin, and told Vic to hold Ray's elbow as firmly as he could. Father pulled hard on Ray's hand, gently felt the broken bones and eased the ends into place, improvised a splint, and drove Ray to the Soudan Hospital.

The doctor congratulated him. "You saved at least three weeks of healing time with your quick action. I couldn't have set the bone better myself." He put a cast on Ray's arm, and both Ray and the Model T were out of commission during haymaking time. And Vic was gone.

᪄᪄᪄᪄᪄᪄᪄᪄᪄᪄

The evening before the Fourth of July, Vic resorted to his old tactics for wheedling the use of the family car. He and Eino were itching to go to the wide-open towns of Gilbert and Virginia. But Father's "*Ei!*" was adamant. He was not about to risk his new car with teenagers, especially not during the wild holidaying of "Forchuly."

Vic sat on the stairs, saunaed and polished to a ruddy Finnish glow. He tried every tactic he could think of. He offered to observe a curfew. Talked about the haymaking season, when he had always been an indispensable worker. About the nice girls—

cousins, really—they wanted to take out. The fact that "Everybody else is going." Father's "*Ei!*" got firmer and angrier.

Vic finally sighed, stood up, and said to Eino, "Guess we'll just go play cards with Matt." They slouched out, looking defeated. After the family went to bed, I heard Mother weakly remonstrating with Father, but they did agree on one thing—Eino was not a suitable companion for Vic; he was a card-carrying Communist.

Father woke up in the night when he heard the horses in the yard. Someone had left the gate open. He looked in the garage; the car was gone. He lit the Aladdin lamp just as Vic was coming home, lights out, motor as silent as possible. Before Father could catch him, Vic highlighted it to the little space above the sauna and spent the rest of the night there.

"When the family drove away to Tower for the Fourth, I went in and changed clothes and took off," he told me years later. "I stowed away in Duluth on a package freighter *Jack*, of the Poker Fleet and wound up in Buffalo. The captain got me a job on the docks stevedoring, but after three weeks I quit and started walking home." At sixteen, the pull of home and family was still strong.

Perhaps Father was the only one who fully realized a young man's need to be on his own, make his own decisions, leave home to find whatever adventure and work he might. Vic himself was still ambivalent. Mother still could not accept his rebellion, even though he had demonstrated it in so many ways. He was her firstborn, the companion of that epic fourteen months of pioneering. Perhaps it would have been easier if he had left once and for all instead of coming back again and again, and giving her new but fragile hope.

❈❈❈❈❈❈❈❈❈❈❈

To cheer us up, Father took us on our annual visit to Aunt Hilda in Chisholm as soon as haying was over. He needed a change too. It hadn't been easy to find good workmen to replace two sons at the last minute, and he had had to work even harder than usual.

The visit was a daylong expedition, from milking time to milking time, and we made it every summer. This time, Mother had hardly climbed, last of all, into the car, tied the laces of her Enna Jetticks and twisted her long hair into a bun stuck with large tortoise shell hairpins before she began to fret.

"Maybe Victor would be with us too if you hadn't been so

strict with him," she began. "Who knows where he might be and what's he doing? Maybe he's hungry or sick."

"*Ole hiljaa!*" Father demanded. "He's been gone over three weeks and any time now he'll remember how much better he has it at home."

"But not even a postcard." She sniffled into her damp handkerchief.

Father slowed the car and swore. "*No saatana.* If we aren't going to have a pleasant visit we might as well turn around and go home right now."

From the corner of my eye I saw Mabel praying, and Ray murmuring to Bobby to distract him from the angry voices. I exercised one of my superstitious bits of magic to keep the nose of the Ford pointed toward Chisholm. I counted telephone poles and the swoops of wire between them: 1 swoop . . . 2 swoops . . . if we passed ten telephone poles, Father would pick up speed and go on. Magic, prayer, Father's own desire for a little diversion— something worked, and we continued on our way.

Twenty miles from home we reached Virginia, proudly ballyhooed on billboards as "Queen City of the Range." Nearing Olcott Park, I craned my neck to see the floral beds designed in symmetrical patterns, and the mangy bison that lumbered from corner to corner of his cage. I remembered that three years before, we had parked nearby and walked to the park to join the Midsummer Festival. Father had suddenly told us all to line up in two facing rows along the edges of the sidewalk. Mother saw a policeman sauntering toward us, gently swinging his night stick. She protested, "Oh, Peter, this isn't necessary."

Father took off his hat and told us to stand up straight while the policeman walked by. Bewildered, we obeyed without protest. Father smiled and in the best English he could muster, said, "Good morning, Officer. Nice day."

I felt very embarrassed; it didn't seem at all an "Americanized" thing to do. Probably the sturdy young man was also embarrassed as he strode the gauntlet of chest-out, shoulders-back Hiltunens. But he touched his nightstick to his cap, smiled, and replied, "Yup, fine day for the fun."

Perhaps Father's idea had emerged from childhood memories of the Czarist regime. I had no idea how brutal an oppressive police could be. I never forgot, though, that policemen are to be respected in America. But not feared.

From Virginia we turned west along the narrow ribbon of

concrete, through Mountain Iron and Buhl with their Rexall Drug Stores and Rex Movie Theaters facing the main road. The bleak stretches between mining towns, uphill and down, were dotted with rust-red heaps of slag beside yawning open pits. Scraggly groves of poplar and birch and young pine clung to the sandy soil.

Among the red Burma-Shave signs whose limericks we read out loud, billboards proclaimed that Hibbing boasted "the world's largest open-pit iron mine." Ray, whose cast kept him from the ball game Leo was playing today, laughed and told us, "It's 400 feet deep, and maybe a mile or more around, but when President Coolidge saw it, all he said was, 'That's a big hole.'"

We crossed a lake at the edge of Chisholm and drove to a "location," a mining company suburb beside a railroad track, where Aunt Hilda, actually our great-aunt, kept a boarding house as her sister, our dead grandmother, had done. The clusters of berries on the mountain ash tree that shaded the white frame house—and was traditionally supposed to bring luck to Finnish homes—were already turning orange-red. Tables were set for dinner on the many-windowed veranda, which looked out on the railroad siding where the miners slept in old boxcars.

Stout and red of face, swathed in a huge white apron, Aunt Hilda was so busy putting dinner on the tables, helped by her pretty teen-aged daughters, that she greeted us only with a big smile, and said, "Glad you finally got here." Uncle Emil, in crisp white shirt, black trousers, and gray suspenders, rang the dinner bell. The boarders, in clean Sunday clothes, hair slicked back with wet combs, filed in and sat around the tables. We sat with the Lehto family and helped ourselves to roast chicken, mashed potatoes and gravy, fresh green peas, coleslaw, several kinds of pickles, hot white rolls, and butter.

Possibly because Uncle Emil was such a quiet man, possibly because of all the boarders, we didn't talk much, even after the apple pie and vanilla ice cream had been served. Occasionally someone remarked on the nice weather or the incredibly low prices of cotton cloth and canned goods. Mother told the Lehtos about Hilma's marriage to her John. Mabel chimed in, "And they drove all the way to California."

Mabel and I helped the girls clear the table and wash the dishes. They were in a hurry to finish. "Our beaus are coming, and we have to get dressed."

We followed them upstairs to watch them primp. Aili carefully drew a Cupid's bow around her mouth and fluffed out her blonde curls. Helen pressed in the ridges of her reddish-brown marcelled waves so they would last. I watched with impatient envy as they pointed their toes and drew on—oh, so carefully— their precious pinky-beige silk stockings, rolled the tops around ruffled garters, straightened the seams in back, slipped their feet into high-heeled black patent leather shoes, and buckled the straps across their insteps.

They sauntered nonchalantly downstairs to greet their beaus. Mabel was undaunted by girls as glamorous as movie stars, and followed at their heels. Nor was she shy of the young men; she boldly asked their names.

But I was in awe of these dapper swells. Hair parted in the middle and wetly slicked back, light gray spats over glistening black shoes, white bell bottom trousers and navy blazers, they looked to me exactly like John Held's drawings of Flaming Youth. When each took his girl by the elbow and helped her into the car I thought I could never wait to grow up and experience such glamour. Helen didn't even blush when she climbed into the rumble seat and her stocking tops showed below her soft blue dress.

When Mother was finally able to claim our attention, she led us back upstairs to a bedroom where an ancient woman sat in a rocker, a shawl around her shoulders, a white kerchief tied under her chin.

"Girls, this is my grandmother, your great-grandmother. She's 86."

The old woman peered at us with eyes gone as small and red-rimmed as a chicken's, and mumbled in Finnish through her toothless gums, "*No niin*. Your girls."

I fidgeted. How should one react to a relative so incredibly old, so near the next world? Above all, so strange, so Old Country?

Mother told us to give her a kiss, and as soon as we had touched our lips quickly and lightly to the papery skin of her cheek, we edged away toward the door. I was backing out, half ashamed to find no love in my heart for my great-grandmother, when I stopped, transfixed by the firm advice she was giving my mother.

"You have to be a *good* woman. Don't flirt with other men."

What a crazy notion. Mother was 36. Flappers like Aili and Helen flirted. Not *mothers*.

That was my first and last sight of the woman baptized Mary Elizabeth Wuornus in a Finnish village near the Arctic Circle in the mid-1800s. All that remains is a dim image of an old lady smelling of lemon soap and corn medicine, and her astonishing admonition to my fat, hardworking, respectable mother.

Aunt Hilda and Mother set the table for coffee, and I knew that now they would really talk. Ray had gone to the movies, Bobby was asleep, and Uncle Emil knew how to get us out of the way. He slipped us each a dime.

We ran a couple of blocks to a little candy store. Its paunchy owner put down the Sunday paper and ambled to the counter to see what we wanted. He was in no hurry; he knew we'd take our time.

We had enough for a candy bar—an O Henry or a Baby Ruth—and a bag of bright gooey things. Or maybe a box of Cracker Jack, sticky and delicious. I was always impatient for a prize—a marble, a tiny top, a balloon, a cardboard figure from the funnies. But Mabel slowly savored every bit of caramel-flavored popcorn before she turned the box over and shook it to find her prize.

Sticky fingered, sated with sweets, and my cotton dress no longer crisp, I was glad when Mother said it was time to go home and take care of the cows. We were rather quiet on the way home. Only Ray was talkative; he'd seen a hilarious Charlie Chaplin comedy. I dreamed groggily of some more things for my *ei kun paljo* list: silk stockings and rolled garters, a boy friend with a car with a rumble seat, fluttery chiffon dresses in lilac and blue.

I gave only a passing thought to the grandmother I had always felt deprived of. That great-grandmother wasn't the jolly, singing, loving, bustling woman I had pictured. That was Grandma Mary, whom I'd never seen.

Bobby was tired and cranky, and wanted only Mother's lap. But she had one of her Sunday-trip headaches, so I took him and jiggled and tickled him, and made up silly songs about everything we saw through the car window, until he went limp against my crumpled dress.

❧❧❧❧❧❧❧❧❧❧❧

The rest of that year is somewhat blurred in my memory. Once more a grimy hobo came home. Once more, despite his Fourth of July escapade, Vic was part of the family. He got a job building a big modern barn for Heikki Hiltula, who planned to open a dairy business. Ray went back to Cook High School for his junior year. Leo was in and out with friends, traps, baseball bats, and hockey sticks, his schoolbooks usually unopened.

Mabel and I were good companions despite our spats, and like all the other school kids, could hardly wait for School 40 to be completely remodeled next summer.

Bobby was Father's shadow, tagging along everywhere, learning more about woods and fields and Father's comings and goings than I ever did. He recalled being very frightened when Father went to a meeting at the Communist Hall to collect the premium for their fire insurance policy, and hearing angry voices shouting, "Revolution now! Down with the capitalists now!"

Father comforted Bobby. "Don't worry about them. They're just a little crazy right now, but it will all straighten out. We'll get a new President who will fix things up." He went right on leading the community Farmer's Club, phone company, and consumer's co-op, and providing entertainment and enlightenment at parties and meetings.

And Mother was still our Rock of Gibraltar. Always there, always busy, always welcoming visitors and wanderers, always ready with a funny memory or a verse or two from the Bible or a well-known poem, almost always available for a warm hug and a whispered confidence.

✖✖✖✖✖✖✖✖✖✖✖

But not always content with her lot. There was the episode of the measles and the stew. The measles were a present from Christmas visitors. Vic was away, Ray in school, but from Leo on down to Bobby, Mother had four feverish, coughing, fretful kids.

One gray January Sunday morning Father told our workman, Otto Niemi, to look after the horses, and skiied down the road and up the hill to Miettunens. For some reason, Mrs. Miettunen and the children spent that winter at her old home, and their house had become a meeting place for card players, especially from early Sunday morning till well into Sunday night.

Otto murmured "*Voi, voi,*" as he watched Father ski away. He washed the dishes and swept the floor, and brought us drinks of water and cool washcloths for our foreheads. But Mother still had the milking and cooking and separating to do.

She cut up, with vicious strokes, potatoes, carrots, onions, and venison, threw them into our big stewpot with a casual handful of spices, and left them cooking when she went to the barn.

Mother had lowered the shade and forbidden us to read. I

wished Father were there to rock Bobby and croon to him, and bring us drinks of water and turn our pillows over to the cooler side. If Otto could see Mother's plight and help, why couldn't Father? He had always said that wasn't the Finnish way; men's and women's work were totally different spheres of action. He had never cooked or swept a floor, and the only time he milked was when Ray was born on the homestead land, and then the cow put her dirty foot into the pail.

Mother had told Mabel and me about her rebellion against husbandly dominance when she was young and had two small boys. Early one summer afternoon, her work done, she took them along through the woods to visit the Makelas, whose daughters were good friends. Father came home earlier than usual and was upset when he didn't find her at home. When she returned, just before coffee time, he raged at her for not staying at home like a good wife.

"If I feel like visiting a neighbor when my work is done," she retorted with spirit, "I will go and visit. I'm no Mrs. Juntunen, who doesn't dare even walk across a field to visit her sister without *Jussi*'s permission!" She won her point—that time.

Around noon Mother served Otto some stew and offered it to those of her patients who had any appetite. Then, grim-faced, she put on her wraps, grabbed the handle of the stewpot, and strode determinedly along the road and up the hill to Miettunens.

Four surprised men looked up from their cards as she opened the door, clumped in, and banged the pot down in the middle of the table, cards or no cards.

"If you can't even come home to eat, much less help me with a houseful of sick kids, then stay here. There's your dinner." And she whirled out again.

I heard her, laughing but still angry, tell Otto about it. Feverish and drowsy, I let my thoughts wander. Of course Mother was right; I wouldn't want to be left with all the work and sick kids either while my husband went off to have fun. Father, I knew, would be embarrassed and angry, and perhaps would give her the silent treatment.

For the first time I began to count the years until I would graduate from high school and leave home, maybe for college. There was no way I could achieve anything on my *ei kun paljo* list if I stayed on the farm.

Darn these measles! I wanted to read. Not think.

Hammer and Sickle

As times got worse, and the newspapers told of spreading misery and protest, Vic seldom read a paper without an outburst of anger.

"There goes Henry Ford again. Listen: 'There is plenty of work to do if people would only do it.' What bullshit! Does he think grown men would rather stand in bread lines than work at regular jobs? And sleep on park benches with newspapers to cover them —'Hoover blankets'?"

Vic had a hard time finding a good job himself. The box factory in Tower had closed down. Heikki's barn was finished. There was an occasional job of road building or repair. But nothing steady, nothing with a future.

He worked hard on the farm when his labor was badly needed for making hay or cutting firewood. And he sang as he worked: not the patriotic or sentimental old American or Finnish songs, but new ones, like "Work and pray, Night and day; There'll be pie in the sky when you die."

But as long as he remained part of the family, these reactions didn't disturb Mother very much. She was never happier

174

than when all of us gathered for Sunday dinner, when by tacit agreement no one talked politics.

The co-operative movement as a whole remained strong and politically neutral, but the rift with the Finnish Workers' Federation wasn't healed for some years. A Communist store and hall were established in Embarrass. As the depression deepened, thousands of Finns left the disappointing Golden Land for the Soviet Union, which had appealed to Finnish lumbermen to come and work in the Karelian forests, in a society without depressions. Listening to grownups talk, I was aware of these things, but I was much more concerned with my own affairs. Then sharp awareness was forced on me, right at home.

※※※※※※※※※※

One sunny washday in May, Mother emptied the men's pants pockets, as she always did. I was hanging the first load of wash on the line when I heard her let out a piercing scream and then break into deep, hoarse sobs. I ran to where she sat on the low step of the sauna, tearing at her hair, shaking, hysterical. Frightened, I couldn't think of any way to comfort her. I had never seen her like this. "Mother, what on earth's the matter?" I managed to ask her.

She thrust a small rectangle of cardboard at me. "This! This! Victor is a Communist. I kept hoping he wasn't, but look at this."

"Victor Hiltunen," the card read, "is a member of the Young Communist League." In the corner was a hammer and sickle.

I tried to think of something to say that would calm her down. "Is that really so terrible, Mother? You know Father always says this is a free country."

I said this only half-heartedly. I thought it was pretty terrible myself, and agreed with Mother just why it was so bad.

"This means he doesn't believe in America, or in God, but in Russia."

Finally her sobs ceased and she pulled herself heavily to her feet. Dad and Vic were entering the house, expecting coffee.

She sent Mabel and me out to push Bobby on the swing. I heard her voice rise hysterically and Father's deeper voice soothing her. If their throats felt like mine, I didn't see how they could even drink coffee that morning. I tried to take pleasure in Bobby's delight as Mabel rhythmically pushed him and recited, "Oh, how

I love to go up in a swing, Up in the air so blue. . ."

I saw Vic and Father leave the house and go back to sawing firewood. Only years later did Vic tell me what happened next. Father asked him calmly, "Have you thought this over carefully, *poika?*"

"Yes, Father, I have."

"Well, I know you would never be a criminal or any other kind of bad person. So there's nothing more to be said."

❧❧❧❧❧❧❧❧❧❧

As the days went by and no more was said, I hardly ever thought of it. Growing up was very much on my mind. Boys were beginning to tease me—which meant they noticed me.

Spring was here; Alma made me a pretty yellow dimity dress. One day during the last week of school, Aili and I ate our lunch seated on rocks in the schoolyard. Some older boys gathered around to talk and joke with us. I thought I must look pretty in my new dress.

Then I became conscious of stares and rib-nudgings and snickers. They were looking at my bosom. I looked down at it. My budding breasts made my dress curve out a little, but—much worse!—in the bright spring sunshine my nipples showed through the thin slip and gauzy dimity.

I crossed my arms over my chest and pretended not to notice, but the boys were merciless. "What is Mavis hiding?" It became a chant: "What is Mavis hiding?" I picked up my lunch pail and fled into the schoolhouse. I heard Aili yell at the boys, "Go climb a tree, you dumb apes!"

That night I told Mother what had happened. We looked up brassieres in the Sears Roebuck catalog and decided to order two for 25¢. Father looked over the order and said, *"Meikäläiset* can't afford to spend money on such nonsense." He crossed them off.

To me that incident has always symbolized the depression. I suppose, though, that Father really thought brassieres were a newfangled American invention, and not for people like us. In any case, I felt angry—and, for the first time, really poor.

Mother found me some white cotton, and I awkwardly made two garments that resembled bras. I hated sewing, and I fumed as I pumped the treadle of our old Singer and thought, "Some day I'll have lots of pretty clothes and store-bought brassieres and I won't have to ask anyone for them."

CX3C3CX3CX3CX3CX3CX3CX

There was a plague of grasshoppers that summer. They whirred up and around us in all directions when we ran through the grass. Mother despaired of her garden; it seemed pointless to have us weed and water the ravaged plants. And we were almost free of baby tending. Bobby was Father's shadow, and went along on errands and chores. So Mabel and I had time to check up on every stage of the transformation of old School 40 into a new, modern building.

Even before school was out, trucks bearing lumber, sacks of cement, kegs of nails, and other building materials left their cargo in the schoolyard. All summer Mabel and Aili and I ran almost daily to join the other kids watching the miracle Henry and Ernest Simonson, with a few workmen, were performing. The teachers had told us that the old school, built in 1914, would be remodeled, but there was little left of it, and a much bigger one was taking shape. The trucks that brought in wonderful new things carried away heaps of rubble and discards.

"There go those hungry old stoves."

"They can't take away the outhouses until the workmen are through."

"Oh, they're taking away all those old desks too."

Perhaps half the schoolkids watched as a huge, deep hole was dug—the basement, which swallowed sacks of cement for walls and floors. Huge, complicated, mysterious apparatuses of furnace, ducts, generator, cables, and wires were installed. The older boys felt very superior, identifying the mysterious tangles of wire and lengths of pipe, naming the odd-shaped bits of metal. Where had country boys learned all that? Maybe from the mail-order catalogs.

Gleaming white lavatories and toilets, and a kitchen sink and tub for the teacherage, appeared. Walls and roof and floors grew to the music of saws and hammers. Henry and Ernie constantly warned us to watch out for nails and broken glass, and shouted, "Hey, you boys, get down from there!" at daring climbers.

CX3CX3CX3CX3CX3CX3CX

One hot day Mrs. Juntunen gave Aili permission to spend the night at our house. On the way home we picked at the gobs of gum on spruce trees and chewed it until it turned pink and we tired of the piney taste. At home we climbed the hay poles and slid down. We dunked and splashed in the brook.

Then we sat cross-legged on the log bridge and watched the dragonflies and water skeeters, and chattered about the wonderful new school. I noticed a red mark on Aili's big toe.

"Did you get a sliver in your toe, Aili?"

She looked at it and answered, a little shamefaced, "No, that's a stamp they put on at every meeting of the Young Pioneers."

I looked closely. It was somewhat blurred, but it was unmistakably a hammer and sickle. I managed to say, "Oh," rather noncommittally. While Mabel went on about the marvels of the school, I silently reflected that Father called Mr. Juntunen "Red Johnny," but was fond of him because he was an *omanpaikkanen*. Just the same, I looked at Aili as if from a great distance, and had to think about how to get through the rest of the day.

"Let's go swing. It's cooler in the shade," I said.

We played until Mother called us to set the table for our good hot weather supper of *laks-lootaa*, a salmon and potato and onion casserole, with lettuce the grasshoppers had spared, and fresh green peas.

We never mentioned the Communist symbol again. The new school gave us plenty to talk about. Huge sheets of glass became windows. Buckets of paint and varnish covered walls and floors. Doors were fitted. We missed very little of the awe-inspiring creation of our new school, even though warnings against touching anything became stronger as the work neared completion.

The very day before school began—Labor Day—we went for a last look, and were the only ones there. Eino Salmela, employed as janitor, showed us around his domain, of which he was to be master as well as slave for many years.

We tiptoed along the shiny floors, flicked light switches, peeked into the new high school room for ninth and tenth grades, with its folding door to the upper grade room that, when opened, created an auditorium. We marveled at the library—shelves, tables, chairs. The high school study hall with chairs with the right arm wide enough to hold a notebook. The drinking fountains, one high, one low, in the hall.

Best of all, oh, best of all, the lavatories, where we ran hot and cold water and flushed the toilets over and over again. Now we, too, would be modern American school kids.

❦❧❦❧❦❧❦❧❦❧❦

Next day—the first day of school—we listened to long lists of rules on how to use the equipment, what the clangor of the electric bells indicated, how to avoid scratching the floors. I was much more interested in the new students from Kugler township, where the school had been closed now that ours had been enlarged. They were mostly Swedish Americans, and one German American; no longer was School 40 all Finnish. Names like Schmidt, Johnson, Hendrickson, were added to the roll call of Salmela, Holappa, Lampi, Hiltunen, and other distinctly Finnish names.

And at recess I took note of the ninth and tenth graders. A high school! I didn't resent the fact that eighth graders had always been the biggest kids, and now as an eighth grader I was overshadowed; life would be much more interesting with teenagers around for school parties and dances and programs. During the first days of school I singled out Vieno Koski as the smartest, Ruth Johnson as the prettiest and sweetest.

And gradually I decided Carol Hendrickson was my new best friend. She laughed at all my jokes. Soon we were staying overnight at each other's houses. I thought her family was very Americanized. Mr. Hendrickson did the milking! They had a two-story house with an upstairs hall and a separate dining room. And they spoke only English, except with the grandmother.

When Carol first told me she had a grandmother, I was envious. Then she took me up to her room one Sunday after we attended the Immanuel Lutheran Sunday School in Tower. The lady was frail and deaf and cranky; she wore a lace cap over her thin white hair. She stayed in her room, full of old-fashioned china and knickknacks and pictures and furniture from Sweden. When she wasn't sitting in her rocker, she puttered about with her cane. The room was stuffy; she always felt cold. She didn't fit my image of a grandmother at all, and I no longer envied Carol. It was her jolly parents and their big house that I really enjoyed.

Only two things really annoyed me at the beginning of that school year. I had a new teacher; Miss Sivula had quit teaching to be married, and married women were not allowed to teach. And when I got my first report card, every grade, for every subject, was 82. I still have it, and I still wonder how that teacher decided to give me those grades. Eventually most of my grades were in the high 90s, but Conduct was rarely above 75, exactly passing.

I was also annoyed with the whispers of the older girls in

the lavatory, just loud enough so we younger ones could hear them complaining—and bragging—about "the monthlies" and "Grandma" coming to visit. Some of them didn't smell very good at those times. Once in a while one had an embarrassing stain on the back of her skirt. But they acted as if they were somehow superior to the rest of us, and yet I envied them their mysterious passage to adulthood. I wanted even that; I would never be satisfied until I had everything there was to be had, short of a broken arm like Bertha Holappa suffered in a fall from our new jungle gym, or the polio our parents talked about in agitated whispers.

With the high school girls as models, I dearly wished I had money for powder, rouge, and lipstick, and even the nail polish that was the latest thing. The Krapu girls set our hair with flaxseed lotion or egg white, but Mabel and I thought our faces looked too pale. So we improvised.

There were always mercurochrome and Vaseline in the house. We took some to our room and blended them carefully, then applied the goo to our lips and cheeks. Not too much, or Father or Mother would send us straight to the wash basin before we could leave the house. I studied magazine ads and added glamorous-sounding cosmetics to the *ei kun paljo* list I carried around in my daydreaming head.

Though at home we still lived without electricity, indoor plumbing, and central heat, modern America came to us via an old radio. Mother bought it second hand with her cream and butter, and Vic installed a battery and fiddled with the three dials until, all of a sudden, we heard a man declaiming, "You are listening to Station WLW, the 100,000 watt transmitter in Cincinnati. And now the news. Thomas Edison, the world famous inventor, died today." It was October 18, 1931.

From that day on, we joined most of the rest of America in laughing at Amos and Andy, and saying "I'se regusted." Ray imitated the crooning of Rudy Vallee. Mabel loved Orphan Annie, and Leo liked Jack Armstrong, the All-American Boy. Father became a devotee of news programs, even though the announcers spoke rapidly, in excited tones, and he had to concentrate to understand. Mother sometimes found hymns and sermons. Sunday evenings became sacred to Jack Benny and Eddie Cantor.

Victor Leaves Home

Christmases were usually happy times at our house. I remember one, however, that threatened not to be happy at all. When Bobby was almost two, Mother was at her wit's end because he got into everything. She was sure no Christmas tree would survive his onslaught. He would snatch, break, even eat the trimmings, and laugh with mischievous glee.

"We might as well forget about a tree this year," she said.

Dismayed, we thought of various schemes. We could put the tree in his playpen.

"He climbs out of it now, so he can climb into it too," Mother pointed out.

When we suggested putting up a small tree on the chest of drawers, she answered, "He'd have a chair up there as quick as a wink."

Mother eyed the strong hook for the Aladdin lamp and said firmly, "The only thing to do is hang it from the ceiling."

"Oh, Mo-o-other! What would people say?"

But Mother was adamant. "That, or no tree at all."

So for that year our tree hung from the ceiling, just out of

Bobby's reach—and, we had to admit, just about as pretty as ever. When visitors came, we made a joke of it. We showed it off before they could make up their minds that the Hiltunens were a little bit crazy.

I remember the following Christmas as a good one too. We had yo-yos, the latest rage, and new dresses for our dolls.

But when I think of Christmas of 1931, a gray pall of sadness settles over me even now.

I was very excited about the school Christmas program. We had a bigger auditorium, and electric lights of many colors on the tree. There were ninth and tenth graders to add glamour to the event. And I was to be the star of a new drill I thought was the most beautiful ever.

Ten girls in short simple white robes each carried a poinsettia leaf. We had each cut a long piece of cardboard into a pointed oval, about arm's length, and covered it with bright red crepe paper. Over and over again, while Miss Laakso played "Glow little glowworm, glimmer, glimmer," we took small dainty steps, formed circles, triangles and figure eights, and tilted our red leaves this way and that.

⛧⛧⛧⛧⛧⛧⛧⛧⛧

On the big night I was proudest of all. Being short paid off for once. At the finale I stood still while the others held their leaves to form a flower around my happy face (brightened with makeup, and my light auburn hair gleaming with the marcelled waves Esther Jokinen had created late that afternoon). I was where I loved to be—at the center of attention. Applauded heartily. Triumphant.

Next day I was still floating in a bubble of happiness when we went to school to clean up. I was thrilled when my idol, Ruth Johnson, a ninth grader, started off saying, "You were so cute last night!"

I thought she was lovely, with her curly blonde hair, blue eyes, dimples, and delicate complexion. But she went on. "Too bad your bloomers were showing. Oh, not much. Just a little bit, when you held the petal up high."

She held her fingers apart almost an inch. When I remember her and that drill now—and those bloomers, pink and new though they were—I still feel a faint warmth of embarrassment in my cheeks.

That humiliation, however, was nothing compared to two events of Christmas vacation. As the older girls sometimes whispered in the lavatory, "Grandma came to visit me." And Victor left home.

❢❣❢❣❢❣❢❣❢❣❢

I think Vic went through the motions: the presents, the dinner, the singing, the family jollity. But for weeks, he hadn't really been part of the family. He was hardly ever home, and we knew he spent a lot of time with the Communists. Several families had left for the Soviet Union. Disillusioned with the Golden Land, they had become convinced that in Russia there was no depression; that the revolution had done away forever with poverty, unemployment, and class differences.

Vic never said in so many words that he too planned to go there, but he sneered at the Hoovervilles, the lack of relief measures for the hungry, and Governor Olson's helpless letters answering pleas for jobs, food, clothes, and shelter with the futile suggestion that they turn to their local churches and agencies. Vic sang "Hallelujah, I'm a bum," and other, more explicit songs about the workers of the world.

Once Ray burst out angrily, "If you think it's so terrible here, why don't you go to Russia?"

"Maybe I will. At least it's a people's democracy, not run by big capitalists."

I couldn't believe he really meant it. He often came out of his deep thoughts and talked with me almost in the old way. He always asked about my teacher and friends, and told me funny stories about things that happened in the box factory in Tower where he briefly worked until it, too, closed its doors.

But the old rapport was missing. We never talked about the most important thing. He probably thought I was too young to understand his ideas and plans. In any case I always tended to steer away from unpleasant topics—"world revolution" in particular. Teachers and parents had so thoroughly steeped me in Americanism that I shunned the thought that he had repudiated it—and so I didn't think much about his rebellion at all.

The day after Christmas his bed was empty. It had often

been empty when he was working or staying overnight with a friend, but this was a really permanent-looking emptiness. Mother cried. Father sat at the window and tapped his fingers, occasionally saying, "*No niin.*" There was no fight, no anger, no recriminations. What had been going to happen just finally did happen.

Little by little, over the next few days, news of him came. The Co-op manager told Father that Vic had charged a warm woolen shirt and socks to his account the day before Christmas. Charlie Peltonen said Vic had bummed a ride to Virginia the day after Christmas and was carrying a packsack. Much later we heard that he had turned up in Duluth, blue with cold from riding on top of a freight car. Eventually, a card came, postmarked Chicago, and another, New York City. Both messages were the same: "Alive."

❊❊❊❊❊❊❊❊❊❊

The last day of the year I woke up early, my stomach aching. It was a new, different, cramping ache, and my thighs felt damp and stuck together. My probing fingers came back to my horrified eyes dark and sticky with blood.

My first impulse was to go to Mother and ask her what to do. But she had never told me anything about "the monthlies." This, then, was what the older girls whispered about in the lavatory, and acted so superior about? I crept out of bed to the clothes chest and found an old white cloth, put on my long underwear, and pinned the cloth back and front. What a horrid feeling! That wad there between my legs, where for twelve years skin had brushed cool and smooth against skin as I walked and ran and sat. I had never felt more alone, more of an alien in the world about which I still had only a sketchy map, stumbling along to find the way that grownups seemed to know but kept a mystery.

Mother noticed that I was cranky and pale. "You need some fresh air. Why don't you walk to the mailbox?"

Still mute and dazed, I struggled into my wraps and went out into the cold gray day. "The curse" had come upon me, and it was no joke that I could see. Putting one foot ahead of the other on the hard frozen ruts of the road, I hated the damp bulkiness "down there."

When I got home, my red eyes and dripping nose looked natural enough for someone who had just been out in the miserable cold. I hurried upstairs to lie face down and let the tears come.

I heard Mother putting Bobby down for a nap. I crept to her bedroom and stood by the stove, head hanging, arms clutching my middle.

Mother finally noticed. She asked, "Don't you feel good, honey?"

I turned and blindly lunged for her arms, burying my head in her soft bosom. "Oh, Mother, I'm bleeding!"

Mother gasped and sat in the rocker, cuddling me on her lap. She murmured, "Poor dear. I thought the girls at school would tell you. I just didn't think it would happen to you so young. But it's natural, and now you will have it every month."

I kept sobbing, hiding my deception in her shoulder. When I quieted down, she explained about "rags" and how to soak them in cold water, and to keep a clean supply on hand.

She picked up a corner of her apron and wiped my face. Gloom cleared as a funny thought struck her. "You poor girl, you're leaking at both ends."

I grinned feebly, stood up, and said, "Okay, I think I'll go and lie down a while."

That ordeal was over. I was glad it was, but two questions nagged at me: Why hadn't I told her I knew—more or less? And why hadn't she explained before?

❧❧❧❧❧❧❧❧❧

Father and Ray tried to inject a little gaiety into our New Year's Eve. They got out the lead and dipper, built up a hot fire, and had each of us hold a little lead in the dipper over the fire until it melted. Then we dropped it into cold water, and Father examined the shape, making funny predictions for the coming year. For example, Ray would win all the events at the county track meet, but his shorts would split during the last one. Ray predicted Mother would have another baby. Father laughed and hugged her, while she blushed. It was true—she did have another, but not that year.

The Matt Holappas had invited us to dinner on New Year's Day. We were glad to escape from our gloomy house.

The day was cold and gray, but windless. After a dinner of pork roast and mashed potatoes with gravy, canned peas, beet pickles, homemade dark bread, and several kinds of cakes and cookies, the children bundled up to go "skating" on the river. I would have made some excuse to stay in and read, but there were only a few Finnish newspapers in the house. I wanted to escape Mother's eyes, which searched my face every little while and lighted up only when I smiled or said something cheerful.

A couple of the boys had skates, but none of the girls did. The boys had swept the ice clear of the dry snow, and it was glassy smooth as we slid around pretending to skate. The other girls teased and shrieked, and pushed one another into the soft snowbanks. I didn't take part.

The image of that river stays with me. The ice was already thick, but so clear that I could see water below it. Dead brown weeds waved as if to say a cold "Goodbye." It fit my mood exactly. That day no one could get me to put on an act and make them laugh. "Come on," they urged, "do your Mickey Mouse or Donald Duck."

I just mumbled, "I have a headache," and skated around slowly, hating the sticky lumpiness between my legs.

When we got home, Mother glanced up toward the boys' room, tightened her lips, and shook her head sadly. She changed to her milking clothes and went to lean her head against Hooveretta's warm flank. I didn't cry for Vic either. I was numb. I tried to cuddle Bobby, but he wiggled out of my lap and began one of his long lonely games, talking with imaginary companions and making chugging noises as he ran his cars around on the warm spot near the bedroom stove. Mabel kept asking me where Victor was. I shrugged off her questions, saying, "I don't know. We'll soon find out."

That night I took a basin of warm water and soap upstairs to try to make myself clean and comfortable. I smelled bad to myself, and was glad there would be sauna the next night. And that Mabel was already asleep.

I snuggled close to her warm, stocky body, and let my thoughts drift. I heard Ray and Leo arguing about whose trap it was that had caught a fine mink. But Vic's loud, jolly, often disputatious voice was missing. The boys' argument seemed to echo thinly in an empty house.

Sleep finally came. I dreamed of the river. Vic was under the ice trying to wave goodbye. He was calling, but the ice was so thick I couldn't hear him. It was so cold that no love came through.

Epilogue

"And then what happened, Grandma?" Heidi and Jana, sixteen years old, want to know.

Life went on. A sister was born in 1933: Betty, the real "caboose," everybody's blonde pet, Father's *"Tassu."*

We grew up, studied, worked, scattered, were married, reflected the passage of years. Only the image of Ray remains young and handsome—the lieutenant who fell in the airborne invasion of the Netherlands in 1944.

In the early 1950s, electricity came to the farm, Bob went to fight in Korea, and Father and Mother gave up the animals and stopped farming.

After Father died in 1956, Mother lived in apartments in Virginia or with my family for months at a time, the perfect grandmother to my children (as well as her ten other grandchildren) that I had always felt so deprived of. Almost every summer she went back to the farm, even when she had to be there alone. Her friends worried about her, but she assured them she felt safe and at home there. If she heard bears snuffling around the gar-

187

Mother and a great-grandson in the rocking chair, summer 1963.

Top: Betty (born in 1933) with Bobby. Bottom: Ray Jacob Hiltunen, 101st Airborne Division, shot down over the Netherlands, September 1944.

bage, she went to get the mail anyway—with two pot lids that she banged together as she marched along and sang "The Battle Hymn of the Republic." She scolded invasive squirrels and talked to friendly frogs, and made her wonderful coffee breads for visitors.

Eventually, as her health failed, I spent summers there too so she would be allowed to stay. City living and her daughters' ministrations had changed her from a dowdy farmer's wife to a smart, slender, attractive elderly lady. She lived to be 88.

After many years in New York, Victor returned west to Superior, Wisconsin, where *Työmies* was now located. He and Leo and their wives were especially fond of the farm, and have spent many summers there. Leo, who managed consumer co-operatives for many years, loved it so much that when he died in 1986, his ashes were scattered over the farm from a little plane.

After many years of living in Europe with her Air Force husband, Mabel settled very near Grandpa's old farm, and taught school. She and Bob, a retired electronics engineer, both have cottages on a beautiful northern lake, and are avid fishermen.

Betty is an accountant and a devoted mother and grandmother. Like all of us except Bob, she has visited Finland and experienced a shock of recognition—"It's so much like home!" The pine woods, the lakes, the aroma of baking in houses bright with rag rugs, the old phrases so common we hardly noticed them as children.

And what about the growing Mavis whose *ei kun paljo* list was heavy with fripperies and material comforts seen in catalogs or the homes of more Americanized friends? I have enjoyed such things in abundance. With the help of wonderful teachers who helped me get scholarships and jobs, I did get to college. There I met the man who made a professional writer of me, pushing and encouraging me until I became self-propelled. Now the things I treasure the most were not even on that wish list sixty years ago—family, love, friendship, this beautiful, fragile Earth—yes, even work. At age eight, one might feel deprived of a grandmother, but beloved grandchildren couldn't begin to be a wish. Now they are my greatest treasure.

Father and Mother never lost their pride in things Finnish, and at the same time became increasingly "Americanized." Home demonstration agents and the Vermilion Neighborly Women's Club continued to teach Mother and her friends the same things millions of other American women were learning in their clubs.

Home in the 1970s, a summer cottage for "Aiti" Hiltunen and her family.

Father was so highly respected as a community leader that he served for years on the English-speaking board of directors of the St. Louis County Fair. They would be astonished now and pleased by two things: the virtual disappearance of the dissensions that gave them so much grief sixty years ago, and the intense interest among the younger generation in all things Finnish.

Victor, faithful to the *Työmies* since soon after he left home, is now president of The *Työmies* Society. The change in the political climate is manifest in one small thing: the paper now publishes church news. And one very important thing: in 1988, conservative old Suomi College conferred on The *Työmies* Society the Heritage Award for its contributions to the preservation and advancement of Finnish-American culture.

Many other publications, societies, clubs, courses, and

festivals also keep alive the love of the Finnish culture, even though among the third generation, few speak the language. Since the time when my father and mother's parents crossed the Atlantic, many bridges have been built between the United States and Finland, helped by jet planes, air mail, and other things not even dreamed of by those people who came here long ago. The ties were never really severed; now they're built back.

❦❧❦❧❦❧❦❧❦❧❦❧❦❧❦

"Going home" now, I rarely think of the dissensions of the 1920s and early 1930s. They have faded like shadows into the turmoil and horror, as well as the urbanization and modernization of the world in the last half century.

Nostalgia is sweet, but painful. On the one hand, I marvel that those immigrants raised large families on that rock-strewn soil, where killing frosts may come in June and again in August. On the other hand, I feel a shiver as if ghosts were vanishing behind each pine tree and decrepit old shed as I look around.

School 40 was torn down years ago. Alders and poplars cover the site of Vermilion Hall. The Co-op has been boarded up

Father, Mother and Mavis on her graduation day from the State University of Iowa, June 3, 1940.

for many years. Ranch-style houses and mobile homes with strange names on the mailboxes now stand along the roads. Only here and there a neighbor from times long gone clings to the old homestead, the remodeled sauna still a ritual gathering place on Saturday nights.

The cabin in which I was born still stands, leaning now and sagging a bit, a summer cottage and hunting lodge for my brothers and their families. Sauna and privy serve their ancient purposes. When the warped and creaking doors of the stable and *puoji* are opened, there is a crude museum of the tools of a time gone by. In a shadowy corner the bulbous silver bowl of the old cream separator gleams softly. Several scythes with beautifully carved oak handles and wicked blades lean against the old axe-hewn log walls. A pair of Father's shoepacks, with upturned toes of soft light suede and sturdy leather uppers, brings a lump to my throat. He used to tread lightly over the crusted snow in them, his feet warm in the wool felt liners.

Sitting in the old rocking chair, sleeping in Father's and Mother's marriage bed, is almost more than I can bear. Though I drink deep of the light air of summer, I cannot stay long. Memories overwhelm me.

Father and Mother in 1954.

And no one "goes home" in winter. The road remains unplowed. Snow weighs down the branches of the pines we climbed. It covers the fields where we made hay and planted potatoes and blankets the barren sites where once stood the red barn, the ice house, the chicken coop, the haymows, the blacksmith shop, and the woodshed. The brook is frozen solid under the snow. Deer and rabbits embroider the lavender-blue shadows with dainty tracks.

Glossary of Finnish Words

Ameriika - Finnish pronunciation of America, stressing first and third syllables.

"Alasti Synnyin" - an old Finnish song, "Naked was I born . . ."

äiti - mother

älä nyt - colloquialism for "Don't tell me!" or "You've got to be kidding." Thus, an expression of surprise or disbelief.

biscuit - a Finnish-American term for sweet egg bread flavored with cardamom, often called *pullaa*, or, in Finglish, *piskettiä*.

ei - no

ei kun paljo - "No, but a lot," Mavis' first words, used in the memoir as expressive of her "wish list."

enkelit - the angels

fellahin - (not a Finnish word; Egyptian peasant)

Finglish - a mixture of Finnish and English, correct in neither language, as in *haussi* for *talo* or house. Comparable to other mixtures such as Spanglish.

Forchuly - Finglish for The Fourth of July.

hanuri - accordion

hieroja - masseuse

hiljaa - be quiet

hulivili - merry fellow

hyi! - phew!

hyvänen aika! - Good heavens!

hyvää päivää - Good morning.

isä - father.

joo - yes.

"Joulu Yö" - "Silent Night" (literally Christmas night).

Joulupukki - the Finnish Santa Claus.

Jumala - God.

Juhannus - Day of St. John the Baptist; Midsummer.

juhla(t) - festival(s).

juusto(a) - cheese; specifically, *uunijuustoa* or "oven cheese."

Kalevala, The - Finland's great epic poem.

kaljaa - non-alcoholic beer, a popular summer drink, especialy at haying time.

kantele - the traditional Finnish lap harp.

kirja - book.

kiuas - sauna stove.

kokko - bonfire, especially the high ones made for Midsummer Night Festivals.

komunisti - Communist.

korppu, korppuja - dry Scandinavian rusks, popular as a coffee bread; sometimes sprinkled with cinnamon and sugar.

körön körön kirkko - a nursery rhyme for bouncing a baby; *"körön"* suggests the up-and-down, back-and-forth motion of a nag, in this case on the way to church.

kulta - gold, dear one (*kultani*, my dear one).

kukkula(t) - hill(s).

laakso(t) - valley(s).

lämmiä - fresh warm milk.

"Meeri," "Meivessi," "Meiboli," "Vikki," "Riku," "Paapi," etc. - Finnicized

versions of American first names: Mary, Mavis, Mabel, Victor, Richard, Bobby.

meikäläiset - our kind of people. Until 1970 I thought it meant only "poor farmers," but a visiting cousin told me it can be used by any group— aristocrats, intellectuals, etc. And that *heikäläiset* means "their kind of people"; *teikalaiset,* "your kind of people." (One of those often-used words not found in my dictionaries.)

miksi - why?

mojakkaa - a hearty meat and vegetable stew; but don't ask for it in Finland, as the name is apparently strictly Finnish-American.

napa - belly button.

Niemi Kalle, Holapan Matti, Hiltulan Heikki - in everyday speech the surname is often mentioned first, commonly as a possessive. Peter Hiltunen, for example, was often called *Hiltu Piiti* or *Hiltu Pekka.*

niinkö? Vai niin? - Is that so? You don't say!

no niin - a frequently used phrase meaning "Well, so . . ." or "Well, then . . ." Often a "filler" while talking.

no saatana - a swearing expression: well, Satan!

"Oi Suomen Maa" "Oh, Finnish Land," the Finnish national anthem.

Ole hiljaa - command, be quiet.

"Oma tupa, oma lupa" - literally, "Own house, own permission." Implies that "In one's own house one can do as one pleases."

omanpaikkasia, omanpaikkanen, omanpaikkaset - different grammatical forms referring to people from the same place as the speaker.

"Paju luokat lonkotellen, rauta kiskot kinkotellen" - difficult to translate, these lines apparently allude to the creaking, squeaking, and complaining of the wood-and-leather horse collar, the iron portions of the harness, and the iron sheaths of the sledge runners burdened with the heavy girls of Piinopirkko.

pappi - clergyman

paskahousu - shit pants (not really vulgar when used as it is most often, referring affectionately to a baby).

pikku piika - little maid; often used affectionately for a helpful small daughter, though a *"piika"* is a servant girl.

poika - boy, son.

Poperikoffi, Stalini, Hooveri - Bobrikov, Stalin, Hoover. The Finnish version of a name changes the "b" to a "p" and adds an "i."

porukka - crowd; humorous reference to a large family.

pujaa - a chicken (or fish) and vegetable stew, made in large quantities for a festive gathering, usually out of doors. A Finnish-American word, possibly borrowed from the Slovenian.

puoji - regional dialect form of *puoti*, shed. We used the *puoji* to keep foodstuffs cool.

pusu - somewhat derogatory term for Slovenians and other East Europeans.

puukko - traditional heavy Finnish knife worn in a sheath at the belt.

Päivää - Good morning; without the "*hyvää*," simply "Morning."

Päivälehti - title of a daily paper published in Duluth during the decades referred to in the book.

rauf! - bowwow!

rippikoulu - confirmation school, an obligatory Lutheran rite of passage at about age 14.

Saako tässä talossa olla yötä? - Could I stay in this house for the night?

sauna - pronounced sow-nah. Finnish-style bath house.

savusauna - smoke sauna; Finnish bathhouse without a chimney, so that soot builds up on the inside surfaces.

siksi - because

sisko - sister

sisu - literally, "guts." To Finns, however, it implies persistence, endurance, willingness to work hard and suffer hardship. Some dismiss the belief that Finns are especially endowed with *sisu* as a chauvinist myth, but all people live by myths, and this has helped sustain Finns through many trials.

sonni - bull

Suomalaisuuden esikuva - example or epitome of Finnish unity.

Suomi - Finland

suonirauta - vein iron, knife for bloodletting

sänky - bed

taivaassa - in Heaven

talo - house

Tassu - pet name for a child, referring to the softness of a kitten's paw.

toiskielinen - literally, other-tongued. One who does not speak Finnish.

Työmies-Eteenpäin - The Worker-Forward - radical leftist weekly paper published since 1903.

turhaa - useless nonsense

uskovainen - believing, a believer (in the Christian faith)

Vaka vanha Väinämöinen - Vainamoinen, old and steadfast, a leading figure in *The Kalevala*.

vihta - sauna whisk, usually of young birch branches.

viili - the Finnish version of whole-milk yogurt. Made from untreated milk, it forms a creamy crust on top.

virsi - hymn

Voi! - Oh! with a connotation of surprise, even disapproval or disappointment.

Thank you to Professor K. Borje Vahamaki, Chair, Department of Scandinavian Studies, University of Minnesota, for his assistance with the glossary.

Mavis Hiltunen (whose birth was registered as Helmi Hiltunen) was born on July 27, 1919, in Vermilion Township, a farm community settled mostly by Finnish immigrants, near Tower, Minnesota, on Lake Vermilion.

Her early life is the subject of this book. She was graduated from Embarrass High School in 1936 and attended Winona State College, Winona, Minnesota, for two years. Her future husband, John Biesanz, persuaded her to transfer to the State University of Iowa, where he got her a scholarship and three jobs. Mavis graduated Phi Beta Kappa and *summa cum laude* in June, 1940; and she and John were married three months later.

They have lived and traveled in many countries, usually accompanied by their three children. Richard is a professor of sociology and anthropology, like his father, and a writer, like his mother. Barry is recognized in many countries as a fine woodworker. Katja, a modern dancer and choreographer, has her own company—the Katja Biesanz Dance Theatre, in California.

With her husband and later with her son Richard and his wife Karen, Mavis has written a number of books: *Costa Rican Life, Modern Society, The People of Panama, Introduction to Sociology, Los Costarricenses,* and *The Costa Ricans.* Their success, especially that of the university textbooks, enabled John to take early retirement in 1971. Since then they have made their home in Costa Rica, where Barry also lives.

Mavis enjoys travel, photography, walking, word games, writing light verse, and a lively correspondence with many friends in several country. She also enjoys her five grandchildren.